RICHARD SANDOVAL

ModernMexicanFlavors

with **David Ricketts**

Photographs by **IGNACIO URQUIZA**

Stewart, Tabori & Chang | New York

**I dedicate this book to
my grandparents,
Felipe and Maruca Sandoval,
who helped nurture my passion
for the foods of Mexico.**

Published in 2002 by
Stewart, Tabori & Chang
A Company of La Martinière Groupe
115 West 18th Street
New York, NY 10011

Export Sales to all countries except Canada, France,
and French-speaking Switzerland:
Thames and Hudson Ltd.
181A High Holborn
London WC1V 7QX
England

Canadian Distribution:
Canadian Manda Group
One Atlantic Avenue, Suite 105
Toronto, Ontario M6K 3E7
Canada

Library of Congress Cataloging-in-Publication Data

Sandoval, Richard.
    Modern Mexican flavors/Richard Sandoval with David
Ricketts; photographs by Ignacio Urquiza.
        p. cm.
    Includes index.
    ISBN 1-58479-161-6
1. Cookery, Mexican I. Ricketts, David. II. Title.

TX716.M4 S263 2002
641.5972--dc21

                                2002070596

Printed in Singapore

10 9 8 7 6 5 4 3 2 1

FIRST PRINTING

PICTURES

Frontispiece: Champiñones Envueltos (see recipe, page 166).

Title page: Zihuatanejo Bay, north of Acapulco, as seen from
the hotel La Casa que Canta, is a calm harbor for sailboats.

Pages 4 to 5: Halibut con Pepitas (see recipe, page 131)
is served on the terrace of the hotel La Casa que Canta,
overlooking Zihuatanejo Bay.

Contents: Modern high-rise buildings encircle the bay at Acapulco.

Contents

A Shock

There I was, standing in the school cafeteria line, ready for my first taste of Mexican food in the United States. I was only thirteen years old and very homesick because I had just moved from my native Mexico to live with my mother in Newport Beach, California. The menu said tacos, and already I could taste them: the soft, warm homemade corn tortillas, filled with wonderfully seasoned shrimp or tuna or spicy chorizo or chicken tinga, and maybe with a tomatillo sauce on the side. I spotted the plate: two curved, hard tortilla shells stuffed with ground beef, shredded lettuce, sour cream, and some sort of red sauce, which they called salsa. I had never seen a hard taco before. In Mexico our tacos were always soft. My homesickness still tugged at me, but on that day a seed was planted that twenty years later would finally come to fruition.

Growing Up

Much of my early life in Mexico centered on good eating. I was born in Mexico City, and on weekends my grandmother and my grandfather—to whom I dedicate this book—would host huge family get-togethers at their house. The food was always special. Grandmother taught me about quesadillas made with homemade tortillas, Mexican cheeses such as cotija and Oaxaca, and all kinds of food from other parts of the world. I loved sleeping overnight at her house, because in the morning Juanita, my grandmother's cook, would serve breakfast chilaquiles—a casserole of tortilla chips, pieces of chicken, tomatillo sauce, and shredded manchego cheese. My grandparents always took me to restaurants, too, so I continued to learn about food in many different ways. Even at that young age, I knew I loved my grandparents . . . and I loved food.

My mother tells me that when I was at home, I usually could be found in the kitchen, eagerly tasting and trying to help, and always, always asking questions.

When I was about ten, I moved to Acapulco, where my father owned a restaurant called Madeiras. Practically every day, I would go there and listen to him talk about the business of running a restaurant: the costs, how to make a profit, and providing good service. Roberto Romo, my father's business partner, was passionate about the ambience of the restaurant. It seemed that he was always having a conversation with the employees,

Tacos de Atún (opposite page; see recipe, page 82) is a delicious example of how I balance flavors and textures in my cooking: richly flavored pan-seared tuna is accented with a spicy Chile de Arbol–Sesame Seed Sauce and a sweet-tart Pomegranate Juice Reduction. The adobo-dressed jícama salad adds a contrasting crunch, as well as a little more heat.

impressing upon them that the restaurant was an extension of his home and that the diners should be treated as friends of the family. I never forgot all those lessons.

Acapulco is famous for its seafood, which only makes sense, since the city is situated right on the Pacific Ocean. Octopus, shrimp, and squid find their way into ceviches; red snapper is delicious when pan-seared; shark is a natural for a quesadilla filling; and on and on. My years growing up in Acapulco are clearly where my strong liking for seafood began. That love of things from the sea is now reflected in my restaurants' menus, and to such an extent that many food critics describe my way of preparing seafood as my special talent. But that's not to say that I don't enjoy cooking pork, beef, and poultry as well and feature them on my menus too.

When I hit my teen years, I moved to a city called Toluca, not far from Mexico City. I was now pretty much on my own, and my main job was being a student. At the same time, I was learning how to be independent and self-sufficient. I didn't have much money, but I would still go out with my friends, and often we'd head for the inexpensive taquerías. I soon discovered the torterías, restaurants that served only sandwiches—but what delicious sandwiches! They were smothered with crema fresca—a kind of Mexican sour cream—beans, salsa, and lots of other ingredients. Even now when I return to the area, I go back to those torterías. The area was a melting pot, since many people had migrated from the countryside to Mexico City in search of work, bringing with them their own styles of regional cooking. I was able to learn a lot about the everyday cooking of Mexico—dishes that were simple but full of flavor.

Tennis and the CIA

My dream as a kid was to be a professional tennis player. When I moved to Newport Beach, I began to spend a lot more time on the courts. During the early eighties, it happened: my dream started to come true. I even toured Europe, playing the professional tennis circuit. As I traveled from country to country in Europe, tasting all the different kinds of food, an interesting change started to take place. The food slowly became more important than the tennis. I finally realized that food was my real passion.

In the late eighties, I enrolled in the Culinary Institute of America at Hyde Park, New York, and there I learned the cooking techniques of classic European cuisine: how to make stocks and sauces, and how to make food look beautiful on the plate. Later I would use those same techniques and the artistry of fine French and Italian cooking to reshape the simple dishes of my grandmother's kitchen—it was my own kind of fusion cooking. I graduated from the CIA in 1991, and I knew it was time to return to Mexico.

Mexico City, like my cooking, is a contrast between the contemporary and the traditional. The Torre Arcos Bosques office building (opposite page) reflects the vibrant modernity of the city.

Behind the Stove

In Acapulco I opened my first restaurant where I was the chef. Actually, it was my father's restaurant, and we named it Villa Fiore—I served Italian food. But I didn't neglect my native cuisine. I was also the chef at my father's other restaurant, Madeiras, where I learned how to make all the basic Mexican sauces—from adobo to mole—and how to put traditional tastes together. Chucho, a chef who worked in the restaurant, was my main mentor. And there was also Señor Huerta, who shared his years of culinary experience with me. Without the two of them, and the invaluable knowledge I gained from them, my own restaurant menus now would be very different.

The more I cooked Mexican, the more I wanted to return to the United States. I wanted to show people in this country what Mexican cooking was about, and that it was not just oversized burritos or plates piled high with rice and beans and tacos. Don't get me wrong—I love rice, beans, and tacos, and they are a very important part of the cuisine of my country. But saying that Mexican cooking is only that would be like saying that in the United States people eat only hamburgers and French fries.

Mercado Libertad, the public market in Guadalajara and one of the largest in Mexico, is a busy place at lunchtime. Workers break for a seafood stew (below), and a young woman uses a tortilla press and a hot griddle to prepare fresh tortillas de maíz blanco, the classic white corn tortillas (opposite page).

I always felt that there were two Mexicos—the one I grew up in and lived in, and the one that people in the United States talk about—and the two are very different. The beginning of my zeal for showing people in this country the true nature of Mexican flavors probably began when I was thirteen years old, standing in that school cafeteria line in Newport Beach, and my passion for food has only increased from year to year.

Modern Mexican Flavors

In 1995 I took the plunge and moved to New York City. I opened a restaurant on the West Side called Savann and created a fusion menu that juggled French, American, and Asian cuisines. A few years later I said to myself, now is the time to shift gears and really focus on Mexican cooking. I found a spot to lease on New York's East Side at First Avenue and Sixty-fourth Street. It was a good-sized space with a couple of empty rooms. I knew I wanted to cook my own brand of contemporary Mexican cuisine, with its exciting combination of flavors and beautifully arranged plates of food. But truthfully, I was a little afraid. I didn't know whether people would welcome this new approach. And I had no idea what to do with the interior space.

The district of Tonalá, just on the edge of Guadalajara in the state of Jalisco, is well-known for its traditional crafts, including handblown glass. An artisan skillfully creates a glass vessel (above), and a glass pitcher is turned and formed while being heated (opposite page).

The artists Roberto Romo and Emilia Castillo, the husband-and-wife team who designed the interior of Maya New York, employ many artisans on their ranch near the town of Taxco, once the site of large silver mines. Silversmiths followed the designs of Emilia to create the water pitchers for the restaurant (opposite page), and wood-carvers in Tlaquepaque near Guadalajara fashioned this detail on a large mirror that now hangs in Maya (below).

At this point, I relied on old friends who had taught me well in the past. Over the years, Roberto Romo, my father's business partner in Mexico and an artist, had shared with me his passion for contemporary Mexican art and crafts. He always believed that restaurants should be designed to feel like a welcoming home, and they should always be full of wonderful art. I telephoned him to ask whether he would help me design my Mexican restaurant in New York City—on a very small budget.

They came to New York, Roberto and his wife, Emilia Castillo, also an artist. When they walked into the space on First Avenue, Emilia spotted a milk crate and dragged it to an archway leading to one of the back rooms. She sat down with her sketch pad on her lap. Roberto stood directly behind her. And they started. They talked back and forth, imagining what the room could look like, and as they talked, Emilia sketched. When they thought they had finally captured the feel of one room, they moved to another and started the process all over again. And that is how Maya was designed—not with detailed architectural renderings but with simple drawings by two gifted artists inspired by the space. And it didn't stop there. Roberto contracted Mexican artisans to handcraft the chairs and paint the interior, while Emilia supervised the silversmiths creating the

tablewear and other decorative touches following her designs. Roberto and Emilia also suggested the name Maya for the restaurant. While they were working on the interior, the Mayan civilization, with all its beautiful visual elements, was always in the back of their minds. I liked the contrast between the ancient Mayan culture and my modern approach to traditional Mexcian cooking. The name stayed.

A few years later, I opened Maya in San Francisco and, within the past year, Tamayo in Denver, which is another expression of love for my native Mexico—Tamayo is a reference to the contemporary Mexican painter Ruffino Tamayo and his colorful canvases.

The Recipes

For more than five years now, through my restaurants I have attempted to be an ambassador for the food of my country. My cooking is rooted in the traditions of Mexico, but I try to put together flavors and ingredients in new and exciting ways that are a reflection of modern Mexico. I always aim for the perfect balance of contrasting flavors, whether it's the tempering of the spicy hotness of chiles by the sweetness of honey and the richness of cream in a Chile de Arbol Sauce (see recipe, page 194) or the pairing of the sourness of tamarind with the sweetness of honey in a vinaigrette. I want people to experience my bold flavors and at the same time wonder what exactly it is they are tasting, since I strive to seamlessly blend the flavors together.

My cooking is not rigidly regional, but it has been influenced by the parts of Mexico where I grew up, mainly Acapulco and the area around Mexico City, including the town of Puebla, the site of an annual mole festival. I've also spent a lot of time in Jalisco in the north Pacific region, where some of the finest cooking in all of Mexico takes place. This is where you find delicious pozole—pork and hominy stews—as well as the world-famous tequilas, an ingredient that adds flavor to much of my cooking.

I hope this book will teach you about Mexican ingredients and flavors, from the dried guajillo chile and huitlacoche to crema fresca and cotija cheese, and how they work together when you recreate my dishes. Even though I've adapted my recipes for the home cook, at first glance some of them may seem a little complicated. However, a lot of the flavored oils that are used in many of the recipes have a long shelf life and so can be made ahead and stored. The same is true for the complex sauces such as the moles and adobos. They can be prepared and stored for a few weeks (and in truth, the older they are, the better they taste).

I always encourage people to try these recipes once and then use them as guidelines for expanding upon their own culinary talents to create new dishes, following their own tastes. Just as beauty lies in the eye of the beholder, so great flavors are in the palate of the creator. So, experiment and be creative.

As the dinner hour approaches at Maya, a staff member makes last-minute adjustments (opposite page): the votive candles on each table are lit, the crisp-starched napkins aligned, and the silverware positioned. Warmly spotlighted glass shelves display some of the handcrafted silver pieces created by Mexican silversmiths in Taxco.

My Flavors

In my style of Mexican cooking, I'm always striving to have three or four contrasting flavors dance about in a delicate balance—for example, the tartness of lemon juice and tomato and the spicy heat of Búfalo sauce playing against the richness of mahi-mahi in a brothy ceviche, or the blending of sweet spices—cinnamon and clove—with the assertive "hotness" of chiles and the bitterness of chocolate in a mole sauce. Tart, sweet, hot, spicy, sour: these are just some of the tastes that I'm continually mixing on my palette.

Notes on Ingredients

Achiote Made from annatto seeds ground with spices, achiote colors dishes a characteristic yellow-orange. It is used frequently in the cooking of the Yucatán peninsula, and particularly in the dish *cochinita pibil*. This traditional preparation involves first brushing a pig with achiote, wrapping it in banana leaves, and then cooking it in a pit. Achiote can also be combined with other ingredients such as chiles, spices, vinegar, and stock to make marinades and sauces. I use an achiote sauce to flavor my Mixiote de Cordero (see recipe, page 160).

Adobo This blend of dried chiles, spices, and herbs, with its fiery sweet taste, is a flavorful concentrate that is an excellent marinade for meats and even seafood, as in my Camarones Adobados (see recipe, page 86). Frequently adobo includes a dash of vinegar, but in my basic recipe I omit it. I like to add the vinegar to the specific dish as I'm making it so I can control the sharpness. By mixing chicken stock or other liquids with the adobo as well as honey and other seasonings, it becomes possible to create lots of different sauces for a wide range of dishes. Commercially prepared powdered adobos are not nearly as flavorful as those that are homemade, but they are not a bad substitute when in a rush. Read the ingredients labels, and avoid those that seem to have a very high sodium content. The powdered adobos can be used dry or can be combined with a little chicken or veal stock or other liquid to make a paste.

Blood Orange Even though these oranges are from the Mediterranean region, I like to use their juice as a flavoring in some of my dishes, especially in sauces for fish (see Huachinango Frito, page 127). This is just another example of how my cooking is inspired by the spirit of Mexican cuisine, but it doesn't necessarily follow the traditional or regional cooking of the country in a strict way. The flesh of the orange is a distinctive deep-red color, with a wonderful sweet-tart flavor that matches well with the heat of the chiles—a balanced heat that characterizes much of my cooking.

Búfalo Sauce I think of this bottled hot sauce, made from chiles, spices, and garlic, as the Mexican equivalent of a Vietnamese or Thai chile sauce. In Mexico, it's very popular as a spicy addition to ceviche. I remember as a teenager dabbing a little Búfalo sauce over shucked fresh clams and oysters that had been seasoned with a squirt of lime juice and a sprinkle of salt. And in case you're wondering, Búfalo has nothing to do with the contents of the bottle—it's just a name.

Cactus Leaves In Mexico we know these leaves as *nopales*. The flat pads or paddles, about 6 to 8 inches long and about 4 or so inches wide, are usually what is available in markets in the United States. To prep them, you must first remove the thorns or nobs by scraping them off with a knife. The whole pads can be grilled or boiled, then cut into strips or cubes, or they can be first cut up and then cooked. The trick is to rinse the cactus well after it has been cut so you can remove the sticky substance that oozes out. It is the same kind of stickiness that you find when you cook okra. I use nopales in salads and as garnishes for other dishes.

Cajeta de Leche de Cabra As a child in Mexico, I would eat this rich, thick caramelized goat's milk just by itself. In the restaurants, I use it for my Crepas de Cajeta (see recipe, page 179), and it's delicious drizzled over ice cream. You can find it bottled in stores specializing in Mexican ingredients.

Canola Oil Since the flavor of canola oil is neutral and doesn't overpower or interfere with other flavors, I use it both in my cooking and for creating the emulsions that I use for garnishing, such as Guajillo Chile Emulsion (see recipe, page 191) and Pasilla Chile Emulsion (see recipe, page 191).

Chayote Long ago a staple for the ancient Mayans, this fruit is becoming more popular in the United States. The chayote has a thin, pale-green skin and a shape that resembles a plump pear. The interior is white with a crisp, watery texture and a soft pit. I like to serve it with fish because of its subtle, sweet flavor.

Cheeses

COTIJA (*ko-TEE-hah*) The aged version of this cheese (*añejo* means "aged") is fairly hard and dry, and its texture and salty flavor are similar to that of Parmesan and dry Monterey Jack. I like to sprinkle cotija over salads, stews, soups, and beans, and often around the rim of a plate or shallow bowl as a garnish.

MANCHEGO (*mahn-CHEH-go*) Derived from the famous cheese of La Mancha, Spain, where it is traditionally made from sheep's milk, this firm, golden cheese has a mellow flavor similar to a slightly aged Jack, but more nutty. It is delicious as a snacking or sandwich cheese, or as an accompaniment to fruit and wine. Manchego also melts well in cooking, as in my queso fundido (see recipe, page 109).

OAXACA (*wa-HA-ka*) A mild, firm white string cheese, Oaxaca has a sweet milk taste and resembles mozzarella. It can be braided or rolled into a ball, and is described by some as reminiscent of the braided silver crafted in the town of Oaxaca, Mexico, where the cheese comes from. I use the cheese as a background flavor and texture, as in Quesadilla Abierta de Camarones (see recipe, page 97). You can substitute mozzarella for Oaxaca.

Chiles, Dried

These provide many of the pleasingly complex flavors experienced in Mexican cooking and are particularly important when it comes to preparing moles and salsas or sauces. When a fresh chile is dried, its flavor becomes much more concentrated, often with an increased intensity of heat. In my recipes, I use mainly whole dried chiles and not the ground dried form.

If you travel throughout Mexico, you'll discover that techniques for using dried chiles vary from cook to cook. Some toast them before soaking; some simmer them in water and then puree them in a blender; and some deep-fry them before incorporating them into a sauce. I like to toast them first, because it brings out the chiles' nutty flavor, adding another dimension to the dish. It's also important not to oversoak the chiles, because that will diminish their flavor.

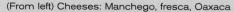

(From left) Cheeses: Manchego, fresca, Oaxaca

To prepare a dried chile, first break off the stem. Then split the chile down the side—this can be done with your fingers or a small knife. Remove the membranes and seeds (or, for a little more heat, leave them in). Be careful not to touch your fingers to your eyes, nose, or lips—or any another sensitive part of your body—while working with chiles. Wash your hands thoroughly when done. Some people prefer to wear rubber gloves when working with chiles.

When buying dried whole chiles, look for ones that are still a little flexible. If they are completely dry and brittle, they shatter very easily and then are harder to work with and more difficult to incorporate into a sauce. Dried whole chiles are usually sold in clear plastic bags, so you can try the bend test. If you store the chiles tightly sealed in a glass container in a cool, dry place, they will usually last up to a year. At home, I like to store them in the freezer, especially if I know I'm not going to use them for a while.

ANCHO Dry a fresh poblano chile, and you'll have an ancho. The heat is mild, and the somewhat sweet flavor is an important component in many moles. Dark maroon, it measures about 2 inches across the top and about 4½ inches down the length.

ARBOL With its bright red skin, this comparatively small chile is about 3 inches long (or a little less) and ¼ inch wide. But don't let the size fool you—it's very hot. On a scale from 1 to 10, I would give it an 8.5. The chile de árbol finds its way into all kinds of table salsas and is very popular in taquerías.

CHIPOTLE The chipotle chile is really just a smoke-dried jalapeño chile. Chipotles are available dried in plastic packets, but probably the most popular way to purchase them is canned in a spicy adobo sauce. Dark brown and about 2 inches long, 1 inch wide, they are very hot—about an 8.5 on my scale of 1 to 10. I take advantage of their distinctive smoky flavor in sauces such as Sweet Chipotle Sauce (see recipe, page 195) and Chipotle Rouille (see recipe, page 201). I often garnish soups with crumbled chipotles not in the sauce.

(From top, clockwise) Chiles: fresh jalapeños, dried chipotles, dried guallijos, fresh poblanos, fresh habaneros, dried moritas, dried chiles de árbol, fresh serranos, dried pasillas, dried anchos, dried piquins, dried casabels, dried guallijos.

GUAJILLO This is the dried chile that is probably the most widely used in households throughout Mexico, because of its abundance in the markets. Usually maroon colored, it's about 5 inches long and 1½ inches wide, and on my heat scale, I would give it a 6 out of 10. I use the guajillo to make a chile emulsion for garnishing some of my plates and as the starting point for my adobo. The chile also adds lots of flavor to meat marinades.

MULATO The sweet, almost chocolate flavor of this dried chile makes it a good choice for moles. Almost black, it's about 5 inches long, and 3 inches wide at the stem end.

PASILLA Very dark in color, this chile is usually about 5 inches long and 1½ inches wide, with a sharp, sometimes almost bitter flavor. On my hotness scale, the pasilla is about a 6.5. Finely chopped pasillas are a popular garnish for tortilla soup and sauces.

Chiles, Fresh

Fresh chiles play a very important role in Mexican cooking. But remember, the level of spiciness varies not only from one type to another but also from one chile to another in the same variety. I suggest always first tasting a little bit of the chile—carefully—so you can figure out the amount to use, depending on how spicy you want your dish to be. Have a glass of milk, a bowl of yogurt, or a piece of bread nearby to tame the heat in your mouth if the chile is too searing. Water will only make your tongue burn worse, since the liquid will spread the chile oil in the mouth.

As chiles ripen, their color will change from green to brighter colors of red and orange. In many recipes, fresh chiles are first roasted, and then peeled. This results in a smoother, softer texture, and a fuller, smoky flavor.

Fresh chiles should be used soon after purchase, but if you need to keep them for a while, store them in the refrigerator, or wrap tightly and freeze.

Poblano

HABANERO This chile is usually orange and resembles a tiny Japanese lantern in shape, about 1½ inches long and 1½ inches wide, and often even smaller. I consider it the hottest of all Mexican chiles. I like to grill or roast them, puree them, and then add just a couple drops of the puree whenever I want to give a dish a boost. Other times, I'll add the chile raw to take advantage of its distinctive taste, as in my Habanero–Red Bell Pepper Reduction (see recipe, page 189), Chive-Habanero Rouille (see recipe, page 201), and Ceviche de Salmón (see recipe, page 36).

JALAPEÑO Usually deep green in color and about 2 to 3 inches long and 1 inch wide, with a rounded end, the jalapeño is frequently used in fresh salsas and is often substituted for the hotter serrano chile. When thinking about chiles, keep this guide to hotness in mind: the thinner the skin of the chile, the hotter the chile will tend to be. The skin of the jalapeño is comparatively thick, which means it is a somewhat mild chile.

Rajas, or vinegar-pickled strips of roasted chiles, a staple in Mexican cooking, are usually made from the jalapeño and often the poblano. My favorite way of eating rajas, which you can purchase canned, is when they are in a ham-and-cheese sandwich. You can also find pickled jalapeños packed in glass jars.

Habanero

POBLANO The shape of the poblano is very recognizable. It's usually 4 to 5 inches long and about 2 to 3 inches wide, with a wide, indented top around the stem, and often a gnarled and misshapen body. The color is very dark green, and its heat is mild, which makes it a versatile chile. In my restaurants, I use the poblano for chile relleno, or stuffed chile—its flavor and texture complement any filling, from cheese to seafood. Other uses include adding it to the stuffing of quesadillas, and sautéing slices with onions and crema fresca. In most preparations, the chile is first charred, then peeled, stemmed, and seeded.

SERRANO Most commonly known in Mexico as chile verde, this chile is very popular in Mexican households and often appears in fresh salsas such as pico de gallo. It's similar in appearance to the jalapeño, but smaller, usually about 2 inches long and ½ inch wide, and deep green. On my hotness meter, it registers 6.5 on a scale of 1 to 10.

Crema Fresca Also known as crema Mexicana, crema fresca tastes like a tangy sour cream and has a similar consistency. You can substitute crème fraîche,

Serrano

Jalapeño

but be sure to stir it well to make it creamy. I would also suggest that if you can't find crema fresca in the refrigerator case in your local market or specialty food shop, try mixing sour cream with a little heavy cream until you get the desired consistency. Crema fresca is great to drizzle on most Mexican finger foods, such as quesadillas, sopes, or tacos. In my restaurants, I use it to garnish many of the dinner dishes, such as Chile Relleno (see recipe, page 72) and Chilaquiles (see recipe, page 146).

Epazote A green herb with narrow, serrated leaves, epazote grows wild in Mexico and in some parts of the United States. I've actually seen it in green markets in New York City. It's used extensively in Mexican cooking, primarily in soups, chopped up in quesadillas, and, most frequently, to flavor black beans. It has a distinctive taste—a combination of lemon and licorice is the best way I can describe it. Once you taste it, you'll always recognize it in a dish. I also like to chop fresh epazote and use it as a garnish with cooked vegetables such as corn, zucchini, and yellow squash. In the United States the dried form is easier to find and, as with any dried herb, you use considerably less than you would if using fresh. A tablespoon or so of dried epazote would be enough for most dishes—and maybe even less.

Huitlacoche

Huazontle This green, which grows wild in Mexico, has long, serrated leaves, and stalks with small seeds. Its flavor is similar to that of broccoli and broccoli rabe, and, in fact, broccoli rabe is a good substitute. A classic way to prepare huazontle is to stuff small pieces of cheese between the stalks, cover the greens with egg whites and flour, and then deep-fry the whole thing and serve it in a tomato broth.

Huitlacoche I like to call this the Mexican truffle, because its flavor is truly unique and somewhat earthy like that of French and Italian truffles. During the rainy season, this fungus, often called corn mushroom, grows naturally on the kernels of fresh corn. It's silvery gray on the outside and black in the inside. It is mostly used in soups or as a stuffing for quesadillas and crepes, and sometimes even in sauces and mashed potatoes. If you can't find it fresh, look for it canned, where it has often been sautéed with onion, garlic, and chiles.

Jícama This vegetable is oval and looks somewhat like a turnip. The outer skin is thin, tough, and beige colored, and is easily removed with a vegetable peeler. The flesh is white and sweet, with a high water content that makes it very crisp, almost like a radish or an apple. In Mexico, jícama is most commonly cut into thin sticks and eaten raw, lightly flavored with lime juice, salt, and

a dusting of chile powder. It's great for salads because of its crispness. In my cooking, I often use it shredded as a salad, as in Tacos de Atún (see recipe, page 82).

Maggi Sauce Maggi is not used a lot in the United States, but I keep it in the kitchen. For me, it is like soy sauce, adding a salty, meaty flavor. I use it mostly for seasoning meats, salads, and soups.

Mole (*MO-lay*) This is the classic Mexican sauce made from blending together dried chiles, spices, nuts, and seeds, and there are as many variations as there are cooks. But one of my favorites, and possibly the most well-known, is the chocolate mole or Mole Poblano (see recipe, page 199), which is most often served with chicken. Its origins are ancient. If people are unfamiliar with this sauce, they often are hesitant to try it when they hear that chocolate and chiles are in the same mixture. But in my experience, once a person has tasted it, he or she is pleasantly surprised and will return again and again to enjoy its subtle complexities.

There are several commercially prepared moles available, my favorite being Doña Maria.

Onion, White Spanish My grandmother cooked with this onion, so it's what I ate growing up. I like its nice crisp texture and clean taste. When I want a slightly sweeter flavor, I'll sometimes cook with Vidalia onions.

Plantain

Tomatillo

Tamarind Pulp is extracted from the pods that grow on the tamarind tree (see photo, page 103), and after being processed it yields a sour, slightly acidic paste. When that paste, which is sold in bricks, is combined with a little sugar, it can be used to marinate shrimp and pork, to glaze duck, or to make a sauce for seafood.

Tomatillo In Mexico, the green tomatillo is almost as popular as the regular tomato. About the size of a lime, it is shiny green and encased in a gray or brown husk. When buying, select those that are firm, with the husk still close to the tomatillo and not very loose. Tomatillos can be stored in the crisper section of the refrigerator for a few weeks. To prepare, first remove the husk and then rinse in warm water to remove any stickiness. I use them raw in some sauces, such as Tomatillo Sauce (see recipe, page 196), as well as cooked as in Pipian Sauce (see recipe, page 200).

Panko I prefer to use these Japanese bread crumbs instead of the finer traditional version, since they are larger, coarser, and dryer, and produce a crunchier texture when fried or cooked in other ways.

Plantain In Mexico we call plantains *plátano macho*, and they are usually twice the size of a regular banana. When they are very ripe, which means the skins are almost black, they can be sliced, sautéed, and then served with rice. Some cooks prefer to use plantains when they are a little less ripe, or almost green, to prepare tostones, a dish in which they are mashed and deep-fried.

Tequila The national drink of Mexico, tequila is made from the blue agave plant and has been part of the Mexican culture for hundreds of years. In addition to its well-known role as a beverage, tequila is wonderful for marinating and also for flambéing. (See Making Tequila, page 40.)

Pomegranate

Pomegranate Round in shape, with a leathery skin that is usually brownish red, this fruit contains lots of seeds in the compartments of its interior. The seeds are held together by a bright red, pulpy membrane that has a tart-sweet flavor. The seeds can be separated out and used to garnish all kinds of dishes—traditionally they are sprinkled over Chile en Nogada (see recipe, page 105). The pomegranate itself can be pressed to extract the juice, which is used for flavoring and in drinks. I use it for my Pomegranate Juice Reduction (see recipe, page 189). Select pomegranates that feel heavy for their size, and if you're not using them right away, you can refrigerate them for up to a month or two. Now the juice is available bottled, which is especially helpful when pomegranates are out of season.

Ceviches and Margaritas

Ceviche

Popular throughout Latin America, especially in Mexico and Peru, ceviche is a light-tasting but intensely flavorful dish that is perfect on its own or as an appetite stimulator at the beginning of a meal. Raw fish is marinated in citrus juice—most often fresh lime juice—with the addition sometimes of onion, tomato, chiles, avocado, and cilantro, to mention just a few of the possible flavorings. The acidity of the citrus juice is what "cooks" the fish. It is essential that the seafood be of the best quality and absolutely fresh.

Ceviche de Callos de Hacha y Calamar

Bay Scallops and Calamari Ceviche with Coconut Milk and Lime Broth

Makes 4 servings

Like so many of my dishes, this one conjures up scenes from my youth. On the edge of the beach, young men climbed the palm trees with their bare hands and feet. They would gather a few coconuts, bring them back down to the ground, and cut them in half with a machete, being careful not to spill any of the flavorful liquid inside. In the same coconut halves, they would mix fresh seafood with the luscious coconut water, a little lime juice, and cilantro—such a wonderful dish and yet so simple, if you don't include climbing a palm tree as part of the preparation.

In a large skillet, cook together the calamari, scallops, and coconut milk over medium heat for 3 minutes. Transfer to a nonreactive large bowl and immediately refrigerate to chill.

Add the remaining ingredients except the coconut halves and cilantro leaves for the garnish. Toss to combine.

To serve Spoon into 4 coconut halves or 4 shallow bowls. Garnish with cilantro leaves.

5 ounces calamari bodies, cleaned and diced
5 ounces bay scallops
1 cup canned unsweetened coconut milk
2 tablespoons freshly squeezed lime juice
1 teaspoon chopped fresh cilantro
1 tablespoon honey
2 fresh serrano chiles, stemmed, seeded, and minced
½ cup chopped red onion
⅓ cup diced fresh pineapple
½ teaspoon salt
¼ teaspoon freshly ground white pepper
4 coconut halves, for serving bowls
Fresh cilantro leaves, for garnish

(Pages 28 to 29) Colorful hammocks (left) are made in the state of Guerrero, along the southern Pacific coast. Many residents of Mexico City escape on weekends to Valle de Bravo (center). The long, green leaves of the blue agave plant (right) are removed in order to harvest the piña, or heart of the plant, from which tequila is made. (Below) Coconuts when halved and hollowed-out make natural serving bowls for ceviche.

Ceviche de Atún

Tuna Ceviche with Tomatillo-Poblano Broth and Mango

Makes 4 servings

TOMATILLO-POBLANO BROTH
6 fresh poblano chiles
6 fresh tomatillos
½ teaspoon hot red-pepper sauce
½ teaspoon Maggi sauce
1 tablespoon freshly squeezed lemon juice
2 teaspoons honey
¼ teaspoon salt
⅛ teaspoon freshly ground black pepper

TUNA
12 ounces fresh tuna steak
½ cup diced mango
¼ cup diced red onion

GARNISH (optional)
4 thin mango wedges
4 Corn Tortilla Chips (see recipe, page 204)

A sampling of three ceviches (opposite page, from left to right): Ceviche de Mahi-Mahi (see recipe, page 35), Ceviche de Salmón (see recipe, page 36), and Ceviche de Atún (see recipe, this page)

This recipe is an unusual departure from the traditional way of making a ceviche. Instead of marinating the fish in fresh lime juice, I make a tomatillo broth, and it's the acid from the tomatillos that "cooks" the fish. The end result is a wonderful combination of flavors.

Tomatillo-Poblano Broth Core and seed the poblano chiles. Cut into chunks. Remove all the papery husks from the tomatillos. Rinse the tomatillos well to remove any stickiness. Cut in half, or quarters if large. In a small bowl, stir together the hot pepper sauce, Maggi sauce, lemon juice, honey, salt, and pepper. In a food processor, working in batches if necessary, puree together the chiles and tomatillos. Force the puree through a medium sieve placed over a nonreactive large bowl, pressing on the solids with a rubber spatula to release the liquid. Discard the solids. Stir the hot pepper sauce mixture into the tomatillo-chile liquid.

Tuna Remove any skin or small bones from the tuna. Cut into ¼-inch cubes. Add the tuna, mango, and onion to the tomatillo broth. Cover and refrigerate 1 hour, stirring occasionally.

To serve Divide the ceviche mixture among 4 martini glasses or shallow bowls. If desired, garnish each with a mango wedge and Corn Tortilla Chip.

Ceviche de Mahi-Mahi

Mahi-Mahi Ceviche with Sweet-and-Spicy Tomato Broth

Makes 6 servings

So much of my cooking is rooted in my childhood in Mexico. I remember, as if it were only yesterday, our family weekends at the beach in Acapulco, where we enjoyed this tomatoey ceviche, a traditional dish of the region. I use the same broth in Vuelve a la Vida (see recipe, page 37). In my version here, I begin the flavoring with a spicy bottled Búfalo sauce—a very picante hot sauce—and then layer on different tomato accents, sweetened with honey and orange juice. It's the acid of the lemon juice that actually "cooks" the fish in this ceviche. (See photo, page 33).

Remove the skin and any small bones from the mahi-mahi. Cut into a ¼-inch dice. In a nonreactive medium bowl, fold together the mahi-mahi and the lemon juice with a rubber spatula. Cover and refrigerate for 30 to 60 minutes, stirring occasionally.

Sweet-and-Spicy Tomato Broth Meanwhile, in a clean nonreactive medium bowl, stir together the ketchup, Búfalo sauce, tomato juice, orange juice, honey, salt, and pepper.

Add the mahi-mahi and lemon juice to the broth, along with the diced tomato, diced onion, and cilantro, folding together with a rubber spatula.

To serve Divide the mahi-mahi mixture among 6 martini glasses or shallow bowls. Garnish each with an avocado slice and a Corn Tortilla Chip, if desired.

¾ pound fresh mahi-mahi
½ cup freshly squeezed lemon juice (about 3 lemons)

SWEET-AND-SPICY TOMATO BROTH
1 cup ketchup
½ cup bottled Búfalo sauce (picante sauce)
½ cup tomato juice
2 tablespoons freshly squeezed orange juice
2 teaspoons honey, or more to taste
½ teaspoon salt
⅛ teaspoon freshly ground black pepper

1 cup diced (¼ inch) tomato
½ cup diced (¼ inch) white Spanish onion
¼ cup thinly sliced fresh cilantro

GARNISH (optional)
¼ of small Haas avocado, pitted, peeled, and cut lengthwise into 4 thin slices
6 Corn Tortilla Chips (see recipe, page 204)

A young fisherman on the beach in Acapulco proudly displays his prize catch of mahi-mahi, or dorado as it's called in Spanish (opposite page). The fish is found in warm waters around the world, and it can weigh up to forty-five pounds.

Ceviche de Salmón

Salmon Ceviche with Habanero Chile and Mustard Seed

Makes 4 servings

10 ounces fresh salmon fillet

½ cup finely chopped purple or red onion

¼ cup diced, peeled, seeded cucumber

1 fresh habanero chile, stemmed, seeded, and finely chopped

1 tablespoon yellow mustard seeds

1 teaspoon black sesame seeds

¼ cup freshly squeezed lime juice (3 limes)

1 tablespoon rice-wine vinegar

1 to 2 teaspoons honey

1 tablespoon chopped fresh cilantro

½ teaspoon salt

⅛ teaspoon freshly ground black pepper

GARNISH (optional)

4 thin strips purple or red onion

The evening lights brighten as twilight descends on Taxco (below), home of the annual national Silver Fair.

Here I play with contrasting textures: crunchy mustard seeds and sweet purple onion, crisp cucumber, and velvety salmon, all underscored by the fiery heat of the habanero chile. It's a great summer dish. (See photo, page 33.)

Remove the skin from the salmon, and carefully pull out any small bones. Cut the salmon into small dice, about ¼ inch. In a nonreactive medium bowl, fold together the salmon, onion, cucumber, habanero chile, mustard seeds, and sesame seeds.

In a nonreative small bowl, stir together the lime juice, vinegar, honey, cilantro, salt, and pepper. Fold into the salmon mixture until evenly coated. Cover and refrigerate until well chilled, about 2 hours, stirring occasionally.

To serve Into each of 4 martini glasses or shallow bowls, spoon a quarter of the ceviche. If desired, garnish with purple or red onion.

Vuelve a la Vida

Octopus and Mixed Shellfish Ceviche with Sweet-and-Spicy Tomato Broth

Makes 4 servings

In my younger days—not so long ago—after a Saturday night of partying in Acapulco's discothèques, a bowl of this ceviche would rescue us from Sunday-morning hangovers— *vuelve a la vida*, in fact, means "back to life."

The spicy tomato broth that I use in this ceviche is one that I also use for my Ceviche de Mahi-Mahi (see recipe, page 35). The real heat comes from the bottled Búfalo sauce. I suggest you first carefully taste a little of the Búfalo sauce before mixing it with the other ingredients so you get an idea of its heat. Then decide whether you want to use a little more or a little less. And remember, you can always temper the heat with the honey.

Sweet-and-Spicy Tomato Broth In a nonreactive medium bowl, stir together the ketchup, Búfalo sauce, tomato juice, lemon juice, orange juice, honey, salt, and pepper.

Seafood In a large saucepan of simmering water, gently cook the octopuses until tender, 30 to 40 minutes. In a large bowl, combine cold water and ice. With a large slotted spoon, remove the octopuses from the water and plunge them into the ice water to stop the cooking. Remove the octopuses from the ice water and blot dry with paper towels. Slice the bodies into rings, and coarsely chop the rest. Set aside.

In a second pot of boiling water, cook the lobster for 5 minutes. With tongs, carefully transfer the lobster from the boiling water to the ice water to stop the cooking. Remove the meat from the shell and cut into small pieces.

In the pot of boiling water, cook the scallops, clams, and oysters for 1 minute. With a slotted spoon, transfer the shellfish to the ice water to stop the cooking. Remove from the ice water and blot dry with paper towels.

Place all the seafood in the spicy broth and let stand for 30 minutes. The ceviche can be made a day ahead and refrigerated, covered.

SWEET-AND-SPICY TOMATO BROTH
1 cup ketchup
½ cup bottled Búfalo sauce (picante sauce)
½ cup tomato juice
2 tablespoons freshly squeezed lemon juice
2 tablespoons freshly squeezed orange juice
2 teaspoons honey
½ teaspoon salt
⅛ teaspoon freshly ground black pepper

SEAFOOD
2 pounds baby octopuses, cleaned
1 live lobster
2 ounces bay scallops
8 clams, removed from the shell
8 oysters, removed from the shell
1 tablespoon freshly squeezed lemon juice
½ cup chopped tomato
¼ cup chopped white Spanish onion
1 tablespoon chopped fresh cilantro

GARNISH (optional)
4 wedges avocado
4 Corn Tortilla Chips (see recipe, page 204)
Chive Oil (see recipe, page 190)

To serve Divide the seafood mixture among 4 martini glasses or shallow bowls. If desired, garnish each with a wedge of avocado, a Corn Tortilla Chip, and Chive Oil.

Mango Margarita

Makes 1 margarita

¼ cup Herradura Silver tequila or other good-quality tequila

1½ tablespoons good-quality sweet-and-sour mix or margarita mix

½ tablespoon freshly squeezed lime juice

6 tablespoons fresh mango puree (see Note)

1 cup ice cubes

1 lime slice, for garnish

Say the word *Mexico* and people almost automatically will think of tequila and margaritas. I love this frozen mango margarita. The first taste always reminds me of Acapulco—the beautiful warm weather, the beaches, and the mango trees everywhere, heavy with ripe fruit. In the United States, when mangoes are not in season you can substitute frozen mango puree.

In a blender, combine the tequila, sweet-and-sour mix, lime juice, mango puree, and ice cubes. Blend until smooth and frothy. Pour into a glass and garnish with the lime slice.

Note To make the mango puree, halve a mango and scoop out the flesh into a small food processor or blender. Puree until very smooth.

Margarita de Oro

Makes 1 margarita

¼ cup Herradura Añejo or Silver tequila or other good-quality tequila

¼ cup good-quality sweet-and-sour beverage mix or margarita mix

2 tablespoons Cointreau liqueur

Juice of 1 lime

1 tablespoon freshly squeezed orange juice

Gran Marnier, for floating on top

Lime slice, for garnish

This margarita is one of our top-shelf cocktails, and at the restaurant we serve it on the rocks. The salt is your choice. Here's a word of advice: using a good-quality tequila from a respected producer, such as the Herradura suggested here, makes a difference not only in taste but also in the morning-after effect.

In a measuring cup, stir together the tequila, sweet-and-sour mix, Cointreau, and lime juice. Pour into a cocktail tumbler. Add ice and float a little Gran Marnier on top. Garnish with the lime slice.

Making Tequila

PROCESSING

Synonymous with Mexico, tequila and its creation dates back to the Spaniards in the sixteenth century, although the Aztecs were fermenting a similar liquid much earlier. Originally tequila was produced only in the state of Jalisco near the town of Tequila, but now production is permitted in four other states.

The making of tequila begins with the maguey or agave plant, and specifically the blue agave, which some say grows best above five thousand feet. Contrary to what many people think, the agave is not a cactus; it is actually a succulent that is a member of the lily family. After the plant has been growing for at least eight years, a jímador, or harvester, uses a coa, a sharp, long-handled tool, to cut out the piña, or heart of the plant. The pineapple-shaped hearts are then slow-roasted, sometimes for as long as two to three days, to release the sugars, and the resulting liquid is then fermented. A double distillation follows, yielding the spirit called tequila. Government regulations control tequila production, including labeling. Only if the tequila is made from 100 percent blue agave is the label allowed to say 100 percent.

Mezcal, the spirit bottled with a worm, should not be confused with tequila. It is made from a variety of agave plants, is not usually double distilled, and does not follow strict production requirements.

GRADES

Blanco tequila is clear, not aged, and is often called silver or white. It's perfect for making margaritas. One of my favorite brands is Herradura Silver. Tequila that is aged in oak for at least two months and up to one year is called **reposado.** It is smoother than the blanco, with more finesse, and is best enjoyed sipped, on the rocks or neat. If the tequila is aged for more than one year, it is labeled **añejo.** These tequilas are like brandy or cognac and deserve to be swirled in a snifter and savored.

A jímador harvests the piña of the blue agave plant (opposite page). Herradura, a producer of quality tequilas, displays some of its antique distillation equipment in the museum at its hacienda near the town of Tequila (above). (left) Rubén Aceves, the international sales manager for Herradura, and I sample a fine añejo tequila aged in oak.

Salads

Ensalada de Berros

Watercress, Hearts of Palm, Orange, and Avocado with Citrus Vinaigrette

Makes 4 servings

2 bunches watercress

1 orange

1 can (7.5 ounces) hearts of palm, drained

1 small avocado

Citrus Vinaigrette (see recipe, page 201)

¼ teaspoon salt

⅛ teaspoon freshly ground black pepper

¼ cup slivered almonds, toasted

Blood Orange Reduction (optional; see recipe, page 189)

(Pages 42 to 43) An arrangement of nopales, or cacti, (left), sit on the terrace of a private residence overlooking Lago Avándaro in Valle de Bravo, a weekend get-away west of Mexico City. The cathedral (center) in Morelia, the capital of the state of Michoacán, is a beautiful example of the Spanish colonial baroque-neoclassic style. Platters of prickly pear fruit (right), ranging in color from light green to purplish-red, are ready for sampling.

Like the common tossed salad in this country, watercress salad with citrus flavors is part of the repertoire of home cooks throughout Mexico. The combination of pungent watercress, crunchy hearts of palms, and rich avocado always seemed to be on the dinner table in the homes of all my friends. It was also a favorite of my grandmother when she cooked for our large family gatherings on weekends.

Rinse the watercress, remove the tough stems, and blot the watercress dry. Then peel the orange and cut into segments, removing the membranes and seeds. Cut 8 hearts of palm in half lengthwise. Cut each into ¼-inch-thick batons, or sticks. Halve, peel, seed, and cut the avocado lengthwise into 12 thin slices.

In a large bowl, combine the watercress, orange segments, hearts of palm, and avocado slices. Add 2 or 3 tablespoons vinaigrette and the salt and pepper, and gently toss together to coat all the ingredients. Add more of the vinaigrette to taste.

To serve In the center of each of 4 chilled large dinner plates, place 2 hearts of palm batons, parallel and 2 to 3 inches apart. Place 2 more batons on top of the first, to make a box. Pile the watercress on top of the box, 2 to 3 inches high. Arrange 3 slices of avocado on each plate at the base of the watercress, in spoke-fashion. Place an orange segment between avocado slices. Garnish the top of the watercress with the almonds. Decorate the plate with dots of the Blood Orange Reduction, if desired. Serve immediately.

Ensalada de Espinaca

Warm Spinach Salad with Bacon, Shiitake Mushrooms, and Chayote with Citrus Vinaigrette and Goat Cheese Crisp

Makes 4 servings

I associate this very simple but very flavorful salad with my father, and the long afternoons we used to spend together at a coffee shop in Acapulco. He'd always order the spinach salad as we sat with our coffee, talking about his restaurant business.

In this salad the thin slices of chayote add a crisp texture, and the deep-fried goat cheese round, a luxurious touch.

In a small skillet, cook the bacon until browned but not crisp, 5 to 6 minutes. Drain on paper towels. Coarsely chop, and set aside.

Shape the goat cheese pieces into disks with rounded corners. Dip in the egg, and then in the panko to coat. Place on waxed paper and refrigerate.

Grill or broil the chayote slices until tender, about 2 minutes per side. Set aside.

In a large skillet, heat the oil. Add the mushrooms and sauté until tender but still firm, 4 to 5 minutes.

In a deep, heavy saucepan, heat 2 to 3 inches canola oil until it registers 375°F. on a deep-fat frying thermometer. Working in batches, add the goat cheese disks. Fry until golden, about 30 seconds; don't overcook or the cheese will begin to melt. With a slotted spoon, transfer the disks to a paper towel–lined baking sheet or plate.

In a small saucepan, heat together the vinaigrette and bacon until warm. In a large bowl, toss together the spinach, mushrooms, onion, chayote, and just enough of the vinaigrette to coat the ingredients.

To serve Remove the chayote slices from the spinach mixture. In the center of each of 4 large plates, pile the spinach mixture. Arrange chayote slices, spoke fashion, on the plate around the spinach. Top the spinach with the goat cheese round. Drizzle with the Chive Oil, if desired, and pass any remaining vinaigrette.

¼ pound sliced bacon

4 ounces firm goat cheese log, sliced into four 1-inch-thick rounds

1 large egg, lightly beaten

½ cup panko (Japanese bread crumbs)

1 chayote, halved, pitted, and sliced lengthwise ⅛ to ¼ inch thick

1 tablespoon canola oil, plus more for frying

1 pound shiitake mushrooms, cleaned, tough stems removed, and caps thinly sliced

½ cup Citrus Vinaigrette (see recipe, page 201)

1 pound baby spinach, washed and dried, tough stems removed

½ red onion, cut into julienne

Chive Oil (optional; see recipe, page 190)

Roberto Romo and his wife Emilia Castillo—the artists who created Maya's interior—designed this beautiful porcelain table with silver inlay (opposite page) to showcase contemporary Mexican silversmithing.

Ensalada de Jitomate

Yellow and Red Tomato Salad with Mizuna and Manchego Cheese

Makes 4 servings

CILANTRO DRESSING
(see Note, opposite page)

2 large egg yolks

1 tablespoon freshly squeezed lemon juice

1 cup canola oil

½ cup crema fresca or crème fraîche, stirred (or sour cream mixed with a little heavy cream)

1 tablespoon sherry-wine vinegar

1 teaspoon honey

1 tablespoon chopped fresh cilantro

½ teaspoon salt

⅛ teaspoon freshly ground white pepper

TOMATO SALAD

2 red medium beefsteak tomatoes

2 yellow medium beefsteak tomatoes

2 ounces goat cheese, softened

¼ teaspoon salt

⅛ teaspoon freshly ground white pepper

½ cup all-purpose flour

½ cup panko (Japanese bread crumbs)

2 large eggs

Canola oil, for frying

¼ pound mizuna, stemmed and cleaned

4 ounces manchego cheese, shaved into strips

Chive Oil (optional; see recipe, page 190)

When I opened Maya San Francisco in 1999, Art, my restaurant manager, kept telling me for about two months that heirloom tomatoes were coming into season and that maybe I should create a menu item using them. I finally listened to him and got to work creating this salad, which I think really shows off tomatoes at their best. It's very important that you pay attention to the quality of the tomatoes, picking ones that are ripe but firm and preferably vine-ripened.

The panko, or Japanese bread crumbs, are coarser than regular dried bread crumbs. When used to coat food and then fried, the result is a crisper and lighter texture.

Cilantro Dressing In a small bowl, whisk together the egg yolks and the lemon juice. Slowly whisk in the oil, a few drops at a time, until the mixture begins to thicken. Continue to whisk in the oil in a thin stream until a mayonnaise forms. Stir in the crema fresca, vinegar, honey, cilantro, salt, and white pepper. (If using crema fresca or crème fraîche, whisk it in a separate bowl to loosen before stirring it into the dressing. Or mix a little sour cream with heavy cream for a substitute.) The dressing can be stored, covered, in the refrigerator for up to 3 days.

Tomato Salad Core the tomatoes and slice each crosswise into ¼-inch-thick slices, for a total of 8 slices of each color tomato. Spread or pat a thin layer of goat cheese on 4 of the yellow tomato slices. Season with salt and white pepper. Spread the flour and panko on two separate sheets of waxed paper. In a shallow bowl, beat the eggs lightly. Dredge each cheese-topped tomato slice with flour, tapping off the excess flour. Dip in the beaten egg, letting the excess drain back into the bowl. Then coat with the panko. Place on a clean sheet of waxed paper.

In a medium saucepan, heat about 2 inches of canola oil until it registers 375°F. on a deep-fat frying thermometer. Working in

batches if necessary to avoid crowding, add the coated tomato slices to the hot oil. Fry until the coating is golden brown, 1 to 1½ minutes. With a slotted spoon or tongs, transfer to a paper towel–lined baking sheet.

In a large bowl, toss the mizuna with just enough dressing to lightly coat the leaves.

To serve In the center of each of 4 large dinner plates or on a platter, arrange the following in a stack: a layer of mizuna, the coated yellow tomato slice, mizuna, 1 red tomato slice, mizuna, 1 yellow tomato slice, mizuna, 1 red tomato slice, and mizuna. Arrange the shaved cheese on the plate around the stack and drizzle with some of the dressing. If desired, decorate with a few drops of the Chive Oil.

Note You can substitute 1 cup bottled mayonnaise for the homemade version in this recipe. If you do, then omit the egg yolks, lemon juice, and the canola oil.

Ensalada de Nopal

Grilled Cactus and Seafood Salad with Apple–Serrano Chile Vinaigrette

Makes 4 servings

Other than the tortilla, no another ingredient reminds me more of Mexico than the nopal, or cactus. I use it in this salad for its crispness and fresh taste. In Mexico, we use the nopal in lots of other dishes, including salsas or sauces, toppings for sopes, and even in soups.

Vinaigrette In a blender, combine the chopped apple and the canola and olive oils. Blend until smooth and the oils are thoroughly incorporated. Add the remaining vinaigrette ingredients. Blend until the mixture is a smooth puree. Adjust the seasoning with salt and pepper, if necessary.

Salad Preheat the broiler or grill. Trim the edges from the cactus paddles. With a chef's knife, scrape or slice off the spiny bumps on both sides of the paddles. Broil or grill the cactus paddles 4 inches from the heat until darkened and tender, about 4 minutes per side. Cut into ¼-inch dice.

In a large skillet, heat the oil over medium heat. Add the mussels and cook, covered, until the mussels open, 2 to 3 minutes, shaking the skillet from time to time. Transfer the mussels to a bowl and keep covered. To the skillet, add the shrimp, calamari, scallops, onion, salt, and pepper, and cook, stirring occasionally, until cooked through, 3 to 4 minutes—be careful not to overcook. Stir in the cilantro. Remove from the heat.

In a large bowl, toss together the arugula and cactus with just enough of the vinaigrette to lightly coat the leaves.

To serve Among 4 bowls or dinner plates, divide the arugula and cactus. Divide the seafood mixture among the plates and drizzle with a little of the vinaigrette. If desired, garnish with the Crisp Tortilla Strips and a drizzle of the Chive Oil.

VINAIGRETTE

2 Granny Smith apples, peeled, cored, and chopped

½ cup canola oil

¼ cup olive oil

2 shallots, chopped

¼ cup balsamic vinegar

1 tablespoon chopped fresh cilantro

1 small fresh serrano chile, stemmed, seeded, and chopped

1 tablespoon honey

1 tablespoon freshly squeezed lime juice

⅓ cup water

½ teaspoon salt

¼ teaspoon freshly ground black pepper

SALAD

2 flat cactus paddles or leaves (about 8 x 4 inches)

1 tablespoon olive oil

12 mussels, scrubbed and debearded

12 large shrimp, shelled if desired

4 ounces calamari bodies, cleaned and cut crosswise into rings

4 ounces bay scallops

2 tablespoons chopped white Spanish onion

½ teaspoon salt

⅛ teaspoon freshly ground white pepper

2 tablespoons chopped fresh cilantro

¼ pound arugula, cleaned and stemmed

GARNISH (optional)

Crisp Tortilla Strips (see recipe, page 204)

Chive Oil (see recipe, page 190)

Soups

Gazpacho de Aguacate

Avocado Gazpacho with Crabmeat

Makes 4 servings

6 large green bell peppers, stemmed,
    seeded, membranes removed,
    and cut into large pieces
1 cucumber, peeled, seeded, and chopped
½ white Spanish onion, chopped
4 very ripe Haas avocados
2 tablespoons freshly squeezed lemon juice
2 teaspoons honey
½ teaspoon salt
⅛ teaspoon freshly ground black pepper

GARNISH
Canola oil, for frying
2 wonton wrappers
¼ pound cooked lump crabmeat
2 tablespoons finely diced red bell pepper
2 tablespoons finely diced green bell pepper
2 tablespoons finely diced peeled jícama

(Pages 52 to 53) The dinner table is set at the
Villa Montaña (left), one of Mexico's finest
small hotels, located in the Santa María hills south
of Morelia, the capital of Michoacán. Chayote
(see page 22) (center) is used in salads and
gratins. Pátzcuaro was the Spanish colonial capital
of the Michoacán region for three centuries,
and many of its plazas, churches, and convents
are built in the colonial style (right).

The inspiration for this refreshing, creamy soup is the traditional Spanish gazpacho, but I've added my own flavorful detour. I blend mashed avocado into the green bell pepper–cucumber base for a velvety texture, and then garnish the whole thing with crabmeat.

In a food processor or blender, working in batches if necessary, combine the green bell peppers, cucumber, and onion, and puree. Scrape into a sieve placed over a bowl, pressing on the solids with a rubber spatula. Discard the solids and set the vegetable juice aside.

Halve the avocados lengthwise. Remove the pits. With a spoon, scoop out the flesh into a clean bowl. Mash to a smooth puree with a handheld blender or in a small food processor. With a handheld blender or whisk, blend the vegetable juice into the avocado. Season with the lemon juice, honey, salt, and pepper. Cover and refrigerate the gazpacho until thoroughly chilled.

Garnish In a medium saucepan, heat about 2 inches of canola oil over medium heat until it registers 375°F. on a deep-fat frying thermometer. Cut the wonton wrappers in half diagonally. Slip them into the hot oil and fry until crisp, about 2 minutes. With a slotted spoon, transfer to a paper towel–lined plate to drain.

To serve In the center of each of 4 shallow soup bowls, place 1 tablespoon crabmeat. Ladle gazpacho into each bowl, dividing equally. Place a wonton-wrapper triangle in the middle of each bowl. Spoon 1 tablespoon crabmeat onto each triangle. Garnish soup with the diced bell peppers and jícama.

Cooling Gazpacho

My first days in a restaurant kitchen were in Acapulco, where the temperature is usually warm, and I needed something on the menu that would cool off my guests after a long day at the beach: my solution was the classic Spanish cold soup. Since then, I've always included a variety of cold soups that begin with the gazpacho as the base.

Gazpacho con Langosta

Gazpacho with Lobster and Mango

Makes 4 servings

During mango season when I was a boy and the streets were literally full of the fruit, I would sometimes get involved in ripe mango fights with my friends—that's probably a tale I shouldn't tell. The strained sweet pepper juice adds a fresh taste to the cold soup, and the lobster a touch of richness.

Gazpacho In a food processor or blender, working in batches, combine the tomatoes, onion, cucumbers, and bell pepper juices. Blend until pureed. Pour through a medium sieve over a bowl, pressing on the solids with a rubber spatula to release the juices. Discard the solids. Stir the lemon juice, Búfalo sauce, salt, and pepper into the juices. Cover and refrigerate until well chilled.

Lobster In a pot large enough to hold the lobster, place the onion and black peppercorns. Fill the pot with water and bring to a boil. Add the lobster, claws first. Cover the pot and cook for 5 minutes. Remove the lobster with tongs and place in large bowl of ice water. When the lobster is cool enough to touch, remove the tail meat and cut crosswise into thin slices. Remove the claw meat and cut into pieces. Set aside.

Croutons Preheat the oven to 350°F. Spread the butter over one side of the bread slices. Place bread, butter side up, on a baking sheet. Bake for 10 minutes, or until crisp and golden brown. Place the goat cheese in a small bowl and whisk until creamy. Spread the goat cheese over the croutons. Set aside.

To serve Into each of 4 wide soup plates, ladle the chilled gazpacho. Add the diced mango. In a medium skillet, heat the Lemon Oil. Add the lobster meat and sauté 2 minutes,

or until cooked through. Place a crouton in the center of each bowl, goat cheese side up. Place a piece of lobster meat on the crouton. If desired, decorate the gazpacho with drops of Chive Oil.

GAZPACHO

2 tomatoes, halved, seeded, and chopped

½ white Spanish onion, chopped

2 cucumbers, peeled, halved lengthwise, seeded, and chopped

2 cups Yellow Bell Pepper Juice (see recipe, page 188)

2 cups Red Bell Pepper Juice (see recipe, page 188)

½ cup freshly squeezed lemon juice (2 to 3 lemons)

2 to 3 drops bottled Búfalo sauce (picante), or to taste

½ teaspoon salt

¼ teaspoon freshly ground black pepper

LOBSTER

½ white Spanish onion, halved

½ teaspoon whole black peppercorns

1 live lobster (about 1¼ pounds)

CROUTONS

2 teaspoons butter, softened

4 slices (¼ inch thick) crusty French bread

1½ ounces soft goat cheese

GARNISH

½ mango, seeded, peeled, and finely diced

1 tablespoon Lemon Oil (see recipe, page 190)

Chive Oil (optional; see recipe, page 190)

Sopa de Tortilla

Tortilla Soup

Makes 4 servings

3 tablespoons canola oil

2 corn tortillas (about 6 inch; see recipe, page 204) or store-bought tortillas

½ cup chopped white Spanish onion

1 clove garlic, finely chopped

1 small dried guajillo chile, stemmed, seeded, and broken into small pieces

1 small dried pasilla chile, stemmed, seeded, and broken into small pieces

½ cup chopped fresh epazote or 2 tablespoons dried epazote

5 plum tomatoes, halved

4 cups Chicken Stock (see recipe, page 186) or canned chicken broth

2 teaspoons freshly squeezed lime juice

½ teaspoon salt

⅛ teaspoon freshly ground black pepper

GARNISH (optional)

½ cup diced avocado

1 ounce manchego cheese, cut into ¼-inch cubes

¼ cup crema fresca or crème fraîche, stirred (or sour cream mixed with a little heavy cream)

1 corn tortilla, diced and fried

1 dried guajillo chile, stemmed, seeded, and crumbled

The story of how I learned to make this most popular of Mexican soups goes back to my father's restaurant, Madeiras, in Acapulco. It was 1991, and I had recently graduated from the Culinary Institute of America in Hyde Park, New York. I was in Mexico spending my first days in the restaurant kitchen alongside Chucho, who was the chef (he is still there creating his wonderful food). It was from watching him that I learned how to make the best Mexican soup I have ever had, which I now serve at my restaurants. But the learning didn't stop there. He also showed me how to create all the basic Mexican sauces. I am forever grateful for having had the opportunity to work with and learn from Chucho.

In a large skillet, heat 2 tablespoons of the oil over medium-high heat. Add the tortillas and fry until crisp, turning over once, 1 to 2 minutes. Transfer the tortillas to paper towels to drain. Break into pieces.

In a large saucepan, heat the remaining 1 tablespoon oil over medium heat. Add the onion and garlic, and sauté until softened and lightly browned, 3 to 4 minutes. Add the dried chile pieces and the epazote, and sauté until the chile pieces are lightly colored on both sides, 30 to 45 seconds. Stir in the tomatoes, tortilla pieces, and stock. Bring to a boil. Lower the heat and simmer, uncovered, over very low heat for 30 minutes.

Working in batches if necessary, pour the soup mixture into a blender and puree. Pour into a medium-mesh sieve placed over a large bowl, and force the solids through with a rubber spatula. Discard any solids left in the sieve.

Season the soup with the lime juice, salt, and pepper.

To serve Spoon the soup into 4 large, shallow soup bowls. If desired, garnish with the avocado and cheese; drizzle a pattern over the top with the crema fresca, and sprinkle with the diced tortilla and guajillo chile.

Sopa de Elote

Roasted Corn Soup with Huitlacoche Dumpling

Makes 4 servings

Since the opening of Maya restaurant in New York City four years ago, this dish has received more compliments than any other. It was created with the help of my sous chef, Antonio, who no longer works with me but whom I still consider a dear friend. The corn soup, which I'm sure will be on the menu for many years to come, is just one of several culinary contributions he made to the restaurant. The flavor secret is to roast the corn first, while it's still on the cob.

SOUP
12 ears corn, with husks
4 cups heavy cream
½ teaspoon salt
¼ teaspoon freshly ground black pepper

HUITLACOCHE DUMPLINGS
4 teaspoons huitlacoche
¼ teaspoon salt
⅛ teaspoon freshly ground black pepper
4 wonton wrappers

Huitlacoche Vinaigrette (see recipe, page 202)

Soup Preheat the grill or broiler. Grill or broil the corn in the husks 6 inches from the heat, turning occasionally, about 20 minutes, or until the husks are charred and kernels are dark brown in spots. When the ears are cool enough to handle, remove the husks and silk. Hold the ears upright, and remove the kernels with a sharp knife by cutting downward along the cob underneath the kernels. Place the kernels in a medium saucepan. Add enough water to the pan to almost cover the corn kernels. Bring to a boil. Lower the heat and simmer until the kernels are very tender, about 20 minutes. Strain the corn kernels, discarding the water.

Working in batches if necessary, puree the corn in a blender or food processor. Using a rubber spatula, force the pureed corn through a medium sieve back into the pan. Discard the solids from the sieve. Add the cream to the saucepan and simmer over low heat for 10 minutes or until desired thickness (the soup should be thin, and not thick like a chowder). Season with the salt and pepper.

Huitlacoche Dumplings While the corn is simmering, prepare the dumplings. In a small bowl, stir the huitlacoche with a fork and season with the salt and pepper. Lay the wonton skins on a flat work surface. Place 1 teaspoon huitlacoche in center of a wonton. Rub the edges of the wonton with a little water. Fold the wonton over the huitlacoche into a triangle to enclose the filling, and press the edges together to seal. Repeat with the remaining wontons and huitlacoche.

In a saucepan of gently boiling water, cook the dumplings until tender, about 1 minute. Remove with a slotted spoon and keep warm.

To serve In each of 4 large, shallow soup bowls, place a dumpling. Ladle the soup into the bowls. Drizzle the vinaigrette decoratively over the top of the soup. Serve immediately.

Tamales

Tamales

Prehistoric in origin, stuffed tamales are one of the most popular dishes in Mexico because they are so versatile—you can fill them with practically anything. Basically a tamale is a corn husk stuffed with a masa, or corn-flour mixture, and then filled with any combination of ingredients, ranging from adobo chicken to sautéed zucchini. There are even sweet versions, such as my Tamal de Chocolate (see recipe, page 170). Once filled, the tamales are steamed and served warm. They can also be prepared ahead and refrigerated for a day or two, and then resteamed or heated in a microwave oven, so you can always have several on hand. Although tamales in Mexico are not usually accompanied by a sauce, I like to create different sauces for different fillings, not only to contrast flavors but also to add moistness to the somewhat dry masa.

Tamales are also one of those foods that can be eaten at any time of day. When I was a child, I remember being at my grandparents' house and waiting anxiously for the sound of the tamale men, who would walk through the neighborhood with their pushcarts, blowing their whistles to let you know that they had hot tamales for sale. As soon as I heard the shrill noise, I'd run to my grandfather, get some money, and then race out to the street, anticipating my first whiff of the fresh tamales as the vendor uncovered the steamer.

Tamal Oaxaqueño

Tamale Stuffed with Shredded Chicken in Mole Sauce

Makes 12 tamales

Unlike other tamales, this one is wrapped in a banana leaf, which imparts a distinctive, almost herb flavor to the masa. Use fresh leaves if you can find them, and cut them into the same size as a corn husk. Otherwise, purchase frozen banana leaves and thaw. Or you can substitute a corn husk.

Chicken Filling In a large pot of simmering water, poach the chicken until just cooked through, 7 to 10 minutes. Remove with a slotted spoon and let cool. Save the liquid for soups or stews. Shred the cooled chicken.

In a large skillet, heat the oil. Add the onion and sauté until softened, about 6 minutes. Add the Mole Poblano and stir in the chicken. Season with the salt and pepper and cook, stirring, for 2 minutes. Set aside.

Tamale Masa In a large bowl, mix together the masa, salt, and baking soda. In a second large bowl, with an electric mixer, beat the lard on medium speed until creamy, 1 minute. In 3 additions, beat in the masa mixture until blended—the mixture will pull away from the sides of the bowl. On low speed, gradually beat in the stock, adding just enough to form a mixture that is not sticky. You should have about 6 cups.

To fill (see photos, page 69) Spread a trimmed banana leaf out on a flat work surface. Pat about ½ cup of the masa mixture over the lower end of the leaf, leaving a ¾-inch border on either side and a 1½-inch border at the top end. Spoon about 3 tablespoons of the chicken filling down the center of the masa mixture. Bring the two long sides of the leaf up and over the masa mixture, so it fits around the filling. Overlap the long sides of the leaf. Fold the end of the leaf up. Repeat with the remaining leaves, masa mixture, and filling. Place the tamales, folded end down, in the insert in a steamer. (The insert needs to be about 4 inches deep.) Add water to the pot to reach a depth of

CHICKEN FILLING
½ pound boneless, skinless chicken breasts
2 tablespoons canola oil
1 cup chopped white Spanish onion
¾ cup Mole Poblano (see recipe, page 199)
½ teaspoon salt
¼ teaspoon freshly ground black pepper

TAMALE MASA
4½ cups instant corn masa mix for tamales
1 teaspoon salt
¾ teaspoon baking soda
3 cups lard or solid vegetable shortening
1½ to 1¾ cups Chicken Stock (see recipe, page 186) or canned chicken broth

12 banana leaves, cut to corn-husk size, or 12 large dried corn husks, soaked and drained

GARNISH (optional)
1 avocado, halved, pitted, peeled, and cut lengthwise into wedges
Crema fresca or crème fraîche, stirred (or sour cream mixed with a little heavy cream)
Chive Oil (see recipe, page 190)

(Pages 60 to 61) Tables await guests at the Villa Montaña in Morelia (left). Many beautiful villages dot the shoreline of Lago Pátzcuaro (center), one of the world's highest navigable lakes, in the state of Michoacán. Silversmiths in Taxco (right) fashion some of the beautiful pieces on display at Maya.

1 to 2 inches. Place the insert in the pot, cover, and steam over low heat for 50 to 60 minutes. (Check the water level from time to time.) When the tamales are done, the leaves can be easily peeled away from the masa. Remove the steamer from the heat and let the tamales remain in the steamer for 2 to 3 minutes to allow the filling to become firm.

To serve For each serving, unwrap a tamale and place in the center of a dinner plate. If desired, arrange the avocado slices on the plates, drizzle the tamales with the crema fresca, and decorate the plates with the Chive Oil.

Tamal de Salmón Ahumado

House-Smoked Salmon Tamale with Roasted Poblano Sauce

Makes 12 tamales

12 large dried corn husks
½ cup hickory chips for barbecuing

ROASTED POBLANO SAUCE
4 fresh poblano chiles
½ cup heavy cream
½ teaspoon salt
¼ teaspoon freshly ground black pepper

TAMALE MASA
4½ cups instant corn masa mix for tamales
1 teaspoon salt
¾ teaspoon baking soda
3 cups lard or solid vegetable shortening
1½ to 1¾ cups Chicken Stock (see recipe, page 186) or canned chicken broth
12 ounces goat cheese (1½ cups crumbled)

SMOKED SALMON
1½ pounds salmon fillet, cut from the center section, skin and bones removed
1 cup Adobo (see recipe, page 192)
3 tablespoons tequila
3 tablespoons canola oil
½ teaspoon salt
¼ teaspoon freshly ground black pepper

Ground árbol chile powder or other chile powder (optional)

Fishermen ready their nets to gather a catch from the ocean waters around Acapulco (opposite page). Halibut, perch, sand bass, triggerfish, and corbinas are just some of the fish that are caught close to shore.

Salmon is a fish that has not been widely available in Mexico, but recently I've seen it appearing more frequently on restaurant menus. I really like the combination here: the corn masa of the tamale, the smoked salmon, and the goat cheese remind me of New York City's traditional bagel with cream cheese and lox.

In a large bowl of warm water, soak the corn husks until softened, about 30 minutes. In a second large bowl of warm water, soak the hickory chips for at least 30 minutes.

Roasted Poblano Sauce Preheat the broiler. Place the chiles on a baking sheet and broil about 4 inches from the heat until charred all over, turning occasionally, 10 to 15 minutes. Transfer the chiles to a brown paper bag, seal, and let stand for 10 minutes. Remove the chiles from the bag. Cut in half lengthwise and remove the stem, seeds, and veins. Peel off the charred skin. In a small saucepan, combine the chiles and the cream and simmer for 10 minutes. Season with the salt and pepper. Pour into a food processor or blender and puree. Return to the saucepan and set aside.

Tamale Masa In a large bowl, mix together the masa, salt, and baking soda. In a second large bowl, with an electric mixer, beat the lard on medium speed until creamy, about 1 minute. In 3 additions, beat in the masa mixture until well blended—the mixture will pull away from the sides of the bowl. On low speed, gradually beat in the stock, adding enough so the mixture is moist but not sticky. You should have about 6 cups. Set aside.

To fill (see photos, page 69) Drain the corn husks and pat dry with paper towels. Spread a corn husk out on a flat work surface. Pat about ½ cup of the masa mixture over the lower, flat end of the husk, leaving about a ¾-inch border on either side and a 1½-inch border at the pointed end. Spoon about 2 tablespoons of the crumbled goat cheese down the center of the masa mixture. Bring

the two long sides of the husk up and over the masa mixture so it fits around the filling. Overlap the long sides of the husk. Fold the pointed end up. Repeat with the remaining husks, masa mixture, and filling. Place the tamales, folded end down, in the insert in a steamer. (The insert needs to be about 4 inches deep.) Add water to the pot to reach a depth of 1 to 2 inches. Place the insert in the pot, cover, and steam over low heat for about 30 to 40 minutes. (Check the water level from time to time.) When the tamales are done, the husks can be easily peeled away from the masa. Remove the steamer from the heat and let the tamales remain in the steamer for 2 to 3 minutes to allow the filling to become firm. Remove the tamales from the steamer.

Smoked Salmon While the tamales are steaming, cut the salmon crosswise into 12 equal portions. In a large bowl, combine the Adobo and tequila. Add the salmon, turning to coat, and let stand for 15 minutes.

Drain the hickory chips and pat dry. Line a wok or large, heavy skillet with foil. Scatter the chips over the bottom. Place a wire rack inside the wok over the chips. Place the wok, with its ring, over a burner. Tightly cover and heat over medium-high heat until the chips begin to smoke, 5 to 10 minutes. Adjust heat as needed.

In a large skillet, heat the oil over medium-high heat. Remove the salmon from the marinade, season with the salt and pepper, and add to the hot skillet. Sear on all sides, about 1 minute. Uncover the wok and place the salmon on the rack, recover, and smoke over medium heat for 5 minutes. Carefully uncover the wok and transfer the salmon to a plate. Remove the wok from the heat, keeping it covered. Gently reheat the poblano sauce.

To serve For each serving, unwrap a tamale and place in the center of a dinner plate. Spoon poblano sauce over the top. Cut a salmon piece diagonally into thin strips, and arrange over the tamale. If desired, sprinkle the plate rim with the chile powder.

Tamal al Chipotle

Chicken Tamale with Sweet Chipotle Sauce

Makes 12 tamales

12 large dried corn husks

CHICKEN FILLING

½ pound boneless, skinless chicken breasts

2 tablespoons canola oil

1 cup chopped white Spanish onion

¾ cup Sweet Chipotle Sauce (see recipe, page 195)

½ teaspoon salt

¼ teaspoon freshly ground black pepper

TAMALE MASA

4½ cups instant corn masa mix for tamales

1 teaspoon salt

¾ teaspoon baking soda

3 cups lard or solid vegetable shortening

1½ to 1¾ cups Chicken Stock (see recipe, page 186) or canned chicken broth

3 cups Sweet Chipotle Sauce (see recipe, page 195)

GARNISH (optional)

1 avocado, halved, pitted, peeled, and cut lengthwise into wedges

Crema fresca or crème fraîche, stirred (or sour cream mixed with a little heavy cream)

Chive Oil (see recipe, page 190)

Tamales—delicious cornmeal mixtures steamed in corn husks—can be found in every region throughout Mexico, but my favorite is from the state of Mexico. Chucho, a chef in my father's restaurant in Acapulco, taught me how to make this tamale. For fewer servings, this recipe is easily divided by two or three. The tamales can also be steamed ahead and then stored in the refrigerator for up to three days. To serve, gently steam again. A good accompaniment is refried beans.

In a large bowl of warm water, soak the corn husks until softened, about 30 minutes. Drain and pat dry with paper towels.

Chicken Filling In a large pot of simmering water, poach the chicken breasts until just cooked through, 7 to 10 minutes. Remove the chicken with a slotted spoon and let cool. Save the cooking liquid for soups, stews, or sauces. Shred the cooled chicken breasts.

In a large skillet, heat the oil. Add the onion and sauté until softened, about 6 minutes. Add the Sweet Chipotle Sauce and stir in the chicken. Season with the salt and pepper, and cook, stirring, for 2 minutes. Set aside.

Tamale Masa In a large bowl, mix together the masa, salt, and baking soda. In a second large bowl, with an electric mixer, beat the lard on medium speed until creamy, about 1 minute. In 3 additions, beat in the masa mixture until well blended—the mixture will pull away from the sides of the bowl. On low speed, gradually beat in the stock, adding enough so the mixture is not sticky. You should have about 6 cups of the masa mixture. Set aside.

To fill (see photos, page 69) Spread a corn husk out on a flat work surface. Pat about a ½ cup of the masa mixture over the lower, flat end of the husk, leaving a ¾-inch border on either side and a 1½-inch border at the pointed end. Spoon about 3 tablespoons of the chicken filling down the center of the masa mixture. Bring the two long sides of the husk up and over the masa mixture so it fits around the filling. Overlap the long sides of the husk. Fold the pointed end up. Repeat with the remaining husks, masa mixture, and filling. Place the tamales, folded end down, in the insert in a steamer. (The insert needs to be about 4 inches deep.) Add water to the pot to reach a depth of 1 to 2 inches. Place the insert in the pot, cover, and steam over low heat for 50 to 60 minutes. (Check the water level from time to time.) When the tamales are done, the husks can be easily peeled away from the masa. Remove the steamer from the heat and let the tamales remain in the steamer for 2 to 3 minutes to allow the filling to become firm.

To serve In a small saucepan, gently heat the Sweet Chipotle Sauce. For each serving, unwrap a tamale and place in the center of a dinner plate. Spoon ¼ cup of the Sweet Chipotle Sauce over the tamale. To garnish if desired, arrange the avocado slices on the plates, drizzle the tamales with the crema fresca, and decorate the plates with the Chive Oil.

Tamal de Langosta

Lobster Tamale with Zucchini Stuffing

Makes 12 tamales

12 large dried corn husks

TAMALE MASA

4½ cups instant corn masa mix for tamales

1 teaspoon salt

¾ teaspoon baking soda

3 cups lard or solid vegetable shortening

1½ to 1¾ cups Chicken Stock (see recipe, page 186) or canned chicken broth

ZUCCHINI FILLING

3 tablespoons canola oil

¾ cup chopped white Spanish onion

6 cups coarsely shredded zucchini with skin on (about 6 medium, 1½ pounds)

¾ teaspoon salt

½ teaspoon freshly ground black pepper

LOBSTER SAUCE

¼ cup (½ stick) butter, at room temperature

¼ cup all-purpose flour

3 cups Lobster Broth (see recipe, page 188)

¾ teaspoon salt

¼ teaspoon freshly ground black pepper

2 teaspoons truffle oil (optional)

4 cups cooked lobster meat (see Boiled Lobster recipe, page 188)

Chive Oil, for garnish (optional; see recipe, page 190)

This tamale is a variation on the popular shrimp tamales served in Sinaloa, on Mexico's northern Pacific coast. There, cooks make the stuffing with very small shrimp with the shells still on, and surprisingly, since the shells are so thin, you hardly notice them at all when you're eating them. In the version here, instead of the shrimp, I garnish the tamale with lobster meat, and for easier preparation, I've substituted shredded zucchini for zucchini blossoms that I usually sauté for the filling. For fewer servings, reduce the recipe by half or a third. The tamales can also be steamed ahead and then stored in the refrigerator for up to three days. To serve, gently steam them again.

Soak the corn husks in a large bowl of warm water until softened, about 30 minutes. Drain and pat dry.

Tamale Masa Meanwhile, in a large bowl, mix together the masa, salt, and baking soda. In a second large bowl, with an electric mixer, beat the lard on medium speed until creamy, about 1 minute. In 3 additions, beat in the masa mixture until well blended—the mixture will pull away from the sides of the bowl. On low speed, gradually beat in the stock, adding enough so the mixture is not sticky. You should have about 6 cups of the masa mixture. Set aside.

Zucchini Filling In a large skillet, heat the oil. Add the onion and sauté over medium heat until softened, about 4 minutes. Add the zucchini and cook, stirring frequently, until the zucchini is softened and most of the moisture has evaporated, 8 to 10 minutes. Season with the salt and pepper. You should have about 2¼ cups of the filling.

To fill (see photos, opposite page) Spread a corn husk out on a flat work surface, or overlap 2 husks if they're small. Spread a ½ cup of the masa mixture over the lower, flat end of

HOW TO STUFF A TAMALE

1 Pat the masa mixture over a soaked corn husk so the mixture is even with the flat end of the husk. Leave a ¾-inch border along the two long sides of the husk and a 1½- to 2-inch border at the top. **2** Spoon the tamale filling down the center of the masa mixture. **3** Bring the two long sides of the husk up and over so the masa mixture fits around the filling. Overlap the sides of the husk. **4** Fold the pointed end of the husk over to seal the narrow end of the tamale. **5** Place the tamales, folded end down, in the insert in a steamer and then cook according to the recipe directions. (Pictured with Tamal al Chipotle filling, see page 66.)

the husk, leaving a ¾-inch border on either side and 1½-inch border at the pointed end. Spoon about 3 tablespoons of the zucchini filling down the center of the masa mixture. Bring the two long sides of the husk up and over the masa mixture, so it fits around the filling. Overlap the long sides of the husk and fold the pointed end up. Repeat with the remaining husks, masa mixture, and filling. Place the tamales, folded end down, in the insert in a steamer. (The insert needs to be about 4 inches deep.) Add water to the pot to reach a depth of 1 to 2 inches. Place the insert in the pot, cover, and steam over low heat for 30 to 40 minutes. (Check the water level from time to time.) When the tamales are done, the husks can be easily peeled away from the masa. Remove the steamer from the heat and

let the tamales remain in the steamer for 2 to 3 minutes to allow the filling to become firm.

Lobster Sauce Meanwhile, in a small bowl, blend together the butter and flour to make a paste. In a small saucepan, bring the Lobster Broth to a simmer. Stir in the flour paste and simmer gently until lightly thickened, about 15 minutes. Season with the salt and pepper, and the truffle oil, if using.

To serve For each serving, unwrap a tamale. In the center of a dinner plate, spoon a pool of the Lobster Sauce. Place a tamale in the sauce, and spoon a little sauce over the top of the tamale. Garnish with the lobster meat and if desired, decorate the plate and sauce with drops of Chive Oil.

Appetizers and First Courses

Chile Relleno

Roasted Poblano Chile Stuffed with Seafood and Gouda Cheese

Makes 4 servings

4 large fresh poblano chiles

SEAFOOD STUFFING
1 tablespoon canola oil
1 small white Spanish onion, chopped
2 cloves garlic, minced
6 ounces shrimp, shelled, deveined, and chopped
6 ounces cleaned calamari, chopped
6 ounces bay scallops, or larger sea scallops, cut into small pieces
½ cup chopped fresh cilantro
¼ teaspoon salt
⅛ teaspoon freshly ground black pepper
½ cup Chile de Arbol Sauce (see recipe, page 194)
½ pound white Gouda cheese, shredded

1 cup Black Bean Puree (see Black Beans recipe, page 186, and Note, below), warmed

GARNISH
Chile de Arbol Sauce (see recipe, page 194)
Crema fresca or crème fraîche, stirred (or sour cream mixed with a little heavy cream)
Chive Oil (optional; see recipe, page 190)

(Pages 70 to 71) A hammock beckons guests in a private home (left) in Valle de Bravo, a short drive west of Mexico City. Handblown glass is fired (center) in one of the many glass workshops in the small city of Tonalá in Guadalajara. The Herradura hacienda (right), near the town of Tequila, is home to one of Mexico's finest producers of tequila.

In Mexico, what goes into a chile relleno varies from region to region. In the towns in the interior of the country, chiles are stuffed with ground meat and cheese, and served with a tomato sauce; on the coasts, the filling is, naturally, seafood. Since I grew up in a coastal city, I like to fill roasted poblano chiles with shrimp, squid, and scallops.

Prepare a grill or preheat the broiler. Grill or broil whole chiles about 4 inches from the heat, turning them over occasionally, until evenly blackened on all sides, 15 to 20 minutes. Place the chiles in a paper or plastic bag and seal. Let stand until cool enough to handle and the skins have loosened, about 15 minutes. Peel off the skins. Cut a slit from the top of each down the side. Remove the seeds and veins. Set the chiles aside.

Seafood Stuffing Preheat the oven to 400°F. In a large skillet, heat the oil. Add the onion and sauté over medium heat until softened, about 5 minutes—don't let the onion brown. For the last 2 minutes, add the garlic. Add the shrimp, calamari, and scallops, and sauté for 2 minutes, or until just cooked through, being careful not to overcook. Add the cilantro, salt, and pepper. Remove from the heat. Add the ½ cup Chile de Arbol Sauce. Spoon the stuffing into the chiles. Place in a baking pan lined with aluminum foil. Top with the cheese.

Bake the stuffed chiles until heated through and the cheese is melted, 10 to 15 minutes.

To serve In the center of each of 4 large salad plates, spoon ¼ cup of the Black Bean Puree. Place a chile on the puree. Drizzle with Chile de Arbol Sauce and then the crema fresca. Garnish with a few drops of the Chive Oil, if desired.

Note You can substitute 1 cup drained, canned black beans pureed with ⅓ cup chicken broth.

Tiritas de Pescado

Pan-Seared Halibut with Tuna Tartare and Jícama Salad in Citrus Vinaigrette

Makes 4 servings

I remember vividly the first time I had a very simple version of this dish. I was in my twenties, playing the tennis circuit in Mexico, and I had just lost in the first round of a tournament in Mazatlán. Discouraged, I headed for the beach to think about whether playing tennis made any sense for me. I sat watching the fishermen bringing in their catch. Right there on the beach they gutted a few of the fish, cut the fillets into small strips or *tiritas*, and then mixed them with fresh lime juice, habanero chiles, and purple onions—a kind of instant ceviche. They offered me a taste, and the memory of that moment is the basis for my recipe here.

HALIBUT
½ pound halibut fillets, cleaned and trimmed
¼ teaspoon salt
⅛ teaspoon freshly ground black pepper
2 teaspoons canola oil
20 fresh cilantro leaves, washed and dried
1 fresh serrano chile, thinly sliced into
    20 pieces

SEASONED ONION
¼ white Spanish onion
1 teaspoon freshly squeezed lemon juice
1 teaspoon bottled Maggi sauce
1 teaspoon honey
¼ teaspoon salt
¼ teaspoon freshly ground black pepper
2 teaspoons canola oil

JICAMA SALAD
1 small jícama
¼ pound fresh tuna, cleaned and trimmed
Huitlacoche Vinaigrette (see recipe, page 202)
¼ pound mâche, washed and dried, tough
    stems removed

GARNISH (optional)
Guajillo Chile Oil (see recipe, page 190)
Citrus Vinaigrette (see recipe, page 201)
Chive Oil (see recipe, page 190)
Black sesame seeds

Halibut Season the halibut fillets with the salt and pepper. In a medium skillet, heat the oil. Add the halibut and quickly sear on both sides, 1 to 2 minutes, leaving the fish very rare in the center. Transfer to a plate and refrigerate until firm, about 15 minutes. Then slice into twenty ⅛-inch-thick pieces, about 3 inches long. Transfer them to a plate lined with parchment paper and refrigerate. Set the cilantro leaves and chile slices aside.

Seasoned Onion Thinly slice the onion. In a small bowl, combine the lemon juice, Maggi sauce, honey, salt, and pepper. In a small skillet, heat the oil over medium heat. Add the onion and the lemon juice mixture, cover the skillet, and cook until the onion is golden brown, about 5 to 8 minutes. Remove from the heat and let cool.

Jícama Salad Peel the jícama and cut into julienne strips. Cut the tuna into small cubes. In a medium bowl, toss together the jícama, tuna, and enough of the Huitlacoche Vinaigrette to moisten. In a separate bowl, toss together the mâche with a little of the vinaigrette to lightly coat.

To serve On each of 4 large salad plates, place 5 pieces of halibut in a star pattern. On the center of each piece of halibut, spoon a little of the seasoned onion, then top with a cilantro leaf and a slice of chile. In the center of each plate, spoon the jícama salad. Top with the mâche. If desired, decorate the plate with dots of the Guajillo Oil, Citrus Vinaigrette, and Chive Oil and sprinkle with the black sesame seeds. Serve immediately.

Calamar Azteca

Calamari in Adobo with Arugula and Plantain Puree

Makes 4 servings

PLANTAIN PUREE

2 yellow-black plantains, soft to the touch
½ cup heavy cream
1 tablespoon freshly squeezed lemon juice
½ teaspoon salt
¼ teaspoon freshly ground black pepper

CALAMARI

2 teaspoons canola oil
12 ounces fresh calamari bodies, cleaned
½ cup Adobo (see recipe, page 192)
2 teaspoons freshly squeezed lemon juice
2 teaspoons honey
¼ cup chopped fresh cilantro
¼ teaspoon salt
⅛ teaspoon freshly ground black pepper
1 bunch arugula, washed and dried, tough
    stems removed

Chive Oil (optional; see recipe, page 190)

A dining room at the Villa Montaña (opposite page) is a colorful background for this beautiful calamari dish.

In my cooking, I love to play with the mixture of sweet and spicy flavors, underscored by a little acidity, and this dish really shows that contrast and balance at work. I sauté the squid with a spicy adobo sauce spiked with dried guajillo chiles, a little honey, and a squirt of lemon juice, and then stuff the squid with slightly bitter arugula. But I don't stop there—the dish is then presented on a sweet puree of roasted plantains and heavy cream.

Plantain Puree Preheat the oven to 350°F. Place the plantains, in their skins, on a baking sheet. Roast for 45 minutes or until very soft to the touch. When cool enough to handle, peel off the skins and cut the plantains into chunks. In a small food processor or blender, blend together the plantains, cream, lemon juice, salt, and pepper. Keep warm.

Calamari In a large skillet, heat the oil. Add the calamari and sauté for 2 minutes. Stir in the Adobo, lemon juice, honey, cilantro, salt, and pepper. Cook for another minute or so, until the calamari is tender—be careful not to overcook. Remove from the heat. With tongs, remove the calamari from the skillet. When the calamari are cool enough to handle, stuff them with the arugula, and cut each body crosswise in half.

To serve On each of 4 large dinner plates, spoon a portion of the plantain puree. Place the halved stuffed calamari on top, standing upright. Spoon the sauce from the skillet around the puree on each plate. Garnish the plate with the Chive Oil, if desired.

Ostiones Sandoval

Baked Oysters Topped with Goat Cheese and Chive-Habanero Rouille,
with Black Bean and Apple Salad

Makes 4 servings

When I sit down (or stand in front of a stove) to create a dish, I often reach back to my youth in Acapulco for a memory of a taste. On Playa Pichilingue—a beach that you could only get to by boat—we would go through dozens of raw oysters and clams that were so fresh they would almost shrink when we sprinkled them with fresh lime juice and the tomato-based spicy Búfalo sauce. The challenge was to re-create those flavors, in a more subtle manner, in the middle of New York City, with oysters lightly cooked. Instead of the Búfalo sauce, I spoon a dollop of a habanero rouille—nothing more than mayonnaise flavored with a very hot habanero chile and lemon juice—on the oysters. A pat of goat cheese brings all the flavors together as I run the oysters under the broiler, and a black bean salad with crisp apples served on the plate helps to clean the palate between mouthfuls of the oyster.

Black Bean and Apple Salad In a medium bowl, combine the beans, apple, onion, tomato, chile, and cilantro. In a small bowl, mix the vinegar and honey. Whisk in the oil until blended. Add the salt and pepper. Add enough of the dressing to the salad to moisten.

Croutons Preheat the oven to 350°F. Spread ½ teaspoon of the butter over one side of each bread slices. Place slices, butter side up, on a baking sheet. Bake until lightly golden and crisp, about 2 minutes.

Oysters Preheat the broiler. Open the oysters and remove them, reserving the bottom shells. In a medium skillet, sauté the oysters over medium heat, turning over frequently, until lightly cooked, about 30 seconds. Place each oyster in a bottom shell. Top each with ½ teaspoon goat cheese, ½ teaspoon Gouda, ½ teaspoon rouille, ½ teaspoon crumbled bacon, and ¾ teaspoon diced tomato. Place on a baking sheet. Broil until heated through and the cheeses are melted, 2 to 3 minutes.

BLACK BEAN AND APPLE SALAD

2 cups cooked Black Beans (see recipe, page 186) or 1 can (19 ounces) black beans, drained

¼ cup diced peeled apple

2 tablespoons chopped white Spanish onion

1 small tomato, halved, seeded, and diced (about ¾ cup)

1 fresh serrano chile, stemmed, seeded, and finely chopped

½ cup fresh cilantro leaves, chopped

1 tablespoon sherry-wine vinegar

2 teaspoons honey

¼ cup canola oil

½ teaspoon salt

⅛ teaspoon freshly ground black pepper

CROUTONS

2 teaspoons butter, softened

4 slices bread (¼ inch thick), from a thin baguette

OYSTERS

12 Blue Point oysters

2 tablespoons firm goat cheese

2 tablespoons grated Gouda cheese

Chive-Habanero Rouille (see recipe, page 201)

3 strips bacon, cooked crisp and crumbled

3 tablespoons finely diced seeded tomato

GARNISH (optional)

Crema fresca or crème fraîche, stirred (or sour cream mixed with a little heavy cream)

Chive Oil (see recipe, page 190)

Arbol chile powder

To serve In the center of each of 4 salad plates, spoon a quarter of the bean salad. Top with a crouton. If desired, garnish with the crema fresca, drizzled in a zigzag pattern over the crouton and salad. Arrange 3 oysters on each plate around the salad. If desired, dot the plate with the Chive Oil, and dust the rim of the plate with the árbol chile powder.

Ostiones Fritas

Pan-Fried Oysters with Parsnip Puree and Jícama Salad

Makes 4 servings

HABANERO–BLOOD ORANGE REDUCTION (optional)

3 cups blood orange juice

½ fresh habanero chile

JICAMA SALAD

1 small jícama, peeled and cut into thin julienne

1 tablespoon freshly squeezed lemon juice

2 teaspoons chopped fresh cilantro

¼ teaspoon salt

⅛ teaspoon freshly ground black pepper

PARSNIP PUREE

6 parsnips (about 1 pound), peeled and diced

2 cups heavy cream

½ teaspoon salt

⅛ teaspoon freshly ground white pepper

OYSTERS

¼ cup uncooked long-grain white rice

16 oysters, in the shell, shucked

¼ teaspoon salt

⅛ teaspoon freshly ground black pepper

2 teaspoons canola oil

Chive Oil (optional; see recipe, page 190)

I'm not particularly a fan of frying oysters, because they taste so great when eaten raw. However, after being served a dish similar to this recipe, in Puerto Vallarta in a cevichería—that's what Mexicans call a small restaurant specializing in seafood and ceviches—I had no choice but to re-create it for the restaurant. And when you taste it, you will know why. The ground-rice coating adds a special crispness, while the flavor of the parsnips is a good complement to the brininess of the oyster and the jícama salad adds a touch of crunchiness.

Habanero–Blood Orange Reduction In a nonreactive saucepan, combine the orange juice and the chile and boil until reduced to ½ cup, about 20 minutes. Discard the chile.

Jícama Salad In a large bowl, toss together the jícama, lemon juice, cilantro, salt, and pepper. Set aside.

Parsnip Puree In a medium saucepan, combine the parsnips, cream, salt, and white pepper. Simmer until the parsnips are tender, 15 to 20 minutes. Drain over a bowl, reserving the cream. Spoon the parsnips into a blender along with half the cream. Puree, adding enough of the remaining cream to form a loose-textured puree. Transfer the puree to a saucepan and keep warm.

Oysters Meanwhile, finely grind the rice in a blender or spice mill. Spread out on a piece of waxed paper. Season the oysters with the salt and pepper. Roll the oysters in the rice to coat. In a large skillet, heat the oil. Add the oysters and sauté until crisp, lightly golden on both sides, and cooked through, 3 to 4 minutes.

To serve In the center of each of 4 dinner plates, spoon about a quarter of the parsnip puree. Top each with about ¾ cup of the jícama salad. On each plate, arrange 4 oysters around the salad. If desired, drizzle the Habanero–Blood Orange Reduction over the plate and dot with the Chive Oil.

Taco de Camarones

Shrimp Taco with Black Bean Puree and Chile de Arbol Sauce

Makes 4 servings

For millions of Mexicans, a taco is a hot, soft corn tortilla stuffed with anything from black beans to meats to seafood, and it's always accompanied by one of hundreds of hot sauces. This is very different from the hard taco shells you usually find at Mexican restaurants in the United States (I never knew that hard shells existed until I came to this country). In this recipe, I've combined a little of both the hard and the soft—it's a shrimp taco that I deep-fry until slightly crisp but still soft.

Shrimp Filling In a large skillet, heat the oil over medium heat. Add the onion and chile and sauté until softened, about 5 minutes. Stir in the shrimp and sauté until just pink, 1 to 2 minutes. Stir in the Adobo and the Tamarind Vinaigrette and cook, stirring, until thickened, about 2 minutes. Stir in the cheese until melted and thoroughly incorporated, and then stir in the cilantro. Remove from the heat and let cool.

Spinach Salad In a large bowl, toss together the spinach and the Chile de Arbol–Tomato Seed Vinaigrette. Set aside.

In a large skillet, heat the tortillas over medium-low for 1 to 2 minutes. Spread half of the shrimp mixture down the center of each tortilla. Roll up each tortilla and secure along the seam with toothpicks.

Heat 3 to 4 inches of oil in a large, deep saucepan until it registers 350°F. on a deep-fat frying thermometer. Working in batches if necessary, slip the filled tortillas into the hot oil. Fry, turning over once, until the tortillas are slightly crisp but still soft, 3 to 4 minutes. With a slotted spoon, remove the tortillas and transfer to a paper towel–lined tray. Cut the tacos diagonally into fourths.

To serve In the center of each of 4 large salad plates, spoon ¼ cup of the Black Bean Puree. Place the spinach salad on top. On each plate, arrange 2 pieces of taco, standing upright on the salad, and spoon the Chile de Arbol Sauce over each. If desired, drizzle with the crema fresca in a zigzag pattern and decorate the plate with the Chive Oil.

Note You can substitute 1 cup drained, canned black beans pureed with ⅓ cup chicken broth.

SHRIMP FILLING

2 tablespoons canola oil

1 cup chopped white Spanish onion

1 fresh habanero chile, stemmed, seeded, and finely chopped

1 pound large shrimp (21 to 30 per pound), shelled, deveined, and cut into 1-inch pieces

¼ cup Adobo (see recipe, page 192)

6 tablespoons Tamarind Vinaigrette (see recipe, page 201)

½ pound Gouda cheese, shredded

½ cup chopped fresh cilantro

SPINACH SALAD

1 small bunch fresh spinach, cleaned, tough stems removed

1 tablespoon Chile de Arbol–Tomato Seed Vinaigrette (see recipe, page 200)

2 flour tortillas (14 inch)

Canola oil, for frying

1 cup Black Bean Puree (see Black Beans recipe, page 186, and Note, below)

Chile de Arbol Sauce (see recipe, page 194)

GARNISH (optional)

Crema fresca or crème fraîche, stirred (or sour cream mixed with a little heavy cream)

Chive Oil (see recipe, page 190)

Tacos de Atún

Pan-Seared Tuna Tacos with Jícama Salad and
Chile de Arbol–Sesame Seed Sauce

Makes 4 servings

JICAMA SALAD

½ small jícama, peeled and cut into thin
   julienne strips

¼ cup Adobo (see recipe, page 192)

1 tablespoon freshly squeezed lemon juice

1 tablespoon honey

2 tablespoons chopped fresh cilantro

½ teaspoon salt

¼ teaspoon freshly ground black pepper

TUNA

1 tablespoon canola oil

12 ounces tuna steak, cut into 4 equal
   portions

¼ teaspoon salt

⅛ teaspoon freshly ground black pepper

4 flour tortillas (about 6 inch), each cut
   into 5 triangles and warmed following
   package instructions

Chile de Arbol–Sesame Seed Sauce
   (see recipe, page 195)

GARNISH (optional)

Pomegranate Juice Reduction
   (see recipe, page 189)

Chive Oil (see recipe, page 190)

Black sesame seeds

I think this is one of the most delicious tuna dishes I have ever made—and also one of the simplest. The sauce, with its toasted sesame seeds and chiles de árbol, nicely complements the rich, strong flavor of the seared tuna, and the jícama salad seasoned with the adobo adds crunch and sharpness. These little tortilla triangles are meant to be picked up with your hands and eaten like a taco.

Jícama Salad In a large bowl, toss together the jícama, Adobo, lemon juice, honey, cilantro, salt, and pepper. Set aside.

Tuna In a large skillet, heat the oil over medium-high heat. Season the tuna with the salt and pepper. Add the tuna to the skillet and sear on each side for 2 to 3 minutes, or until desired doneness. Remove the tuna from the skillet and cut each into 5 portions.

To serve On each of 4 large plates, place 5 tortilla triangles, spoke-fashion. Place a portion of tuna on each tortilla triangle, and top each with a dollop of the Chile de Arbol–Sesame Seed Sauce. In the center of each plate, pile the jícama salad. If desired, decorate the plates with the Pomegranate Juice Reduction and the Chive Oil, and garnish with the sesame seeds.

Camarones al Tequila

Tequila-Marinated Shrimp with Black Bean Pancake, Arugula Salad, and Hibiscus Sauce

Makes 4 servings

Hibiscus, better known in Mexico as Jamaica flower, which grows especially well along the southern Pacific coast in the state of Guerrero, is very much unknown in the food world and in the United States. But once you get hold of it, you will understand what a wonderful ingredient it is to work with. Its slightly acidic flavor adds a refreshing tang to everything from drinks and sherbets to jellies and sauces. I like to brighten seafood dishes with its acidic edge.

The black bean pancakes in this dish are very good on their own as a first course, drizzled with a little crema fresca or topped with one of my sauces (see pages 192 to 197).

Hibiscus Sauce In a large saucepan, combine the flowers, the water, and the honey. Gently boil until most of the liquid has evaporated and the flowers are just covered with liquid, about 45 minutes. Strain over a bowl, and discard the flowers. Return the liquid to the saucepan and continue to gently boil until reduced to a light-syrup consistency, about 25 minutes. Let cool, and then refrigerate to chill.

Black Bean Pancakes In a medium bowl, stir together the Black Bean Puree, egg, and flour until smooth and the consistency of a pancake batter—adjust with flour or bean cooking liquid if necessary. Season with the salt and pepper. In a large skillet, heat the butter. Spoon in 2½ tablespoons batter for each pancake, for a total of 4. Cook for about 2 minutes or until the bottoms are lightly browned. Flip pancakes over and cook for another 1 minute or until cooked through. Transfer to a baking sheet and keep warm.

Arugula Salad In a large bowl, toss together the arugula, lemon juice, salt, and pepper.

Tequila Shrimp Season the shrimp with the salt and pepper. In a large skillet, heat the

butter. Add the shrimp, working in batches if necessary, and sauté until pink, curled, and almost cooked through, about 2 minutes. Carefully add the tequila and tilt the skillet to ignite the tequila. Let the flames die down. Be careful not to overcook the shrimp.

To serve In the center of each of 4 dinner plates, spoon a pool of the hibiscus sauce. Place a bean pancake in the center of each pool. Top each with a mound of arugula salad and 2 shrimp. Dot with Chive Oil, if desired.

HIBISCUS SAUCE

2 ounces dried hibsicus flowers

8 cups water

7 tablespoons honey

BLACK BEAN PANCAKES

½ cup Black Bean Puree (see Black Beans recipe, page 186)

1 large egg, lightly beaten

¼ cup all-purpose flour

¼ teaspoon salt

⅛ teaspoon freshly ground black pepper

2 tablespoons butter, or more as needed

ARUGULA SALAD

1 small bunch arugula, cleaned and stemmed

1 tablespoon freshly squeezed lemon juice

¼ teaspoon salt

⅛ teaspoon freshly ground black pepper

TEQUILA SHRIMP

8 jumbo shrimp (11 to 15 per pound), peeled with tails intact, deveined

¼ teaspoon salt

⅛ teaspoon freshly ground black pepper

2 tablespoons butter

¼ cup tequila

Chive Oil (optional; see recipe, page 190)

Camarones Adobados

Shrimp Marinated in Adobo with Arugula-Mango Salad in Chipotle-Tamarind Vinaigrette

Makes 4 servings

SHRIMP

12 jumbo shrimp (11 to 15 per pound),
　　shelled and cleaned (see Note, below)

¼ cup Adobo (see recipe, page 192)

2 tablespoons butter

ARUGULA-MANGO SALAD

1 small bunch arugula, cleaned and stemmed

¼ cup diced mango

1 teaspoon freshly squeezed lemon juice

¼ teaspoon salt

⅛ teaspoon freshly ground black pepper

GARNISH

Chipotle-Tamarind Vinaigrette (see recipe,
　　page 201)

Chive Oil (optional; see recipe, page 190)

Shrimp marinated in adobo and eaten with fresh tortillas is a popular dish in central Mexico and Michoacán, and was the starting point for this recipe. My own special touch is the arugula-mango salad dressed with a Chipotle-Tamarind Vinaigrette, which balances the sourness of the tamarind, the sweetness of honey, the acidity of sherry-wine vinegar, and the smoky hotness of the chipotle chile.

Shrimp In a large bowl, combine the shrimp and Adobo and refrigerate, covered, for 1 hour. In a large skillet, heat the butter. Add the shrimp and sauté until cooked through, 3 to 4 minutes.

Arugula-Mango Salad While the shrimp are marinating, in a large bowl, toss together the arugula, mango, lemon juice, salt, and pepper.

To serve In the center of each of 4 large salad plates, pile a quarter of the arugula-mango salad. Arrange 3 shrimp around the salad on each plate. Drizzle with Chipotle-Tamarind Vinaigrette and Chive Oil, if using.

Note You may leave the shells on the shrimp for both cooking and serving. At Maya, the shrimp are served with the heads on.

Napoleon de Langosta

Lobster Napoleon with Creamy Goat Cheese and Arugula Salad

Makes 4 servings

The first thing that you will probably ask is, What is a napoleon recipe doing in a Mexican cookbook? It's not as strange as you may think. This dish is based on one called sincronisada, which is two fried corn tortillas stuffed with ham and cheese, like a sandwich. Our family once had a cook named Sipriana, and she made a version that paired seafood with cheese. Years later I still remember how rich and delicious that combination was. As a tribute, I've created my own lobster "sandwich."

Creamy Goat Cheese In a small bowl, mash the goat cheese with a fork. Gradually stir in the half-and-half and Roasted Garlic Puree until smooth. Stir in the honey, salt, and pepper. Set the mixture aside.

Lobster Emulsion In a medium-size saucepan, combine the Lobster Broth and chile. Gently boil until reduced to ¼ cup, about 30 minutes. Remove the chile and discard, and pour the broth into a blender. With the blender running, slowly add the oil until a thick emulsion forms. Blend in the honey and vinegar, adjusting the amounts according to taste.

Crisp Tortillas In a deep, medium saucepan, heat 2 inches of canola oil until it registers 350°F. on a deep-fat frying thermometer. Working in batches to avoid crowding the pan, fry the circles until crisp, 1 to 2 minutes per side. With a slotted spoon, remove the circles to a paper towel–lined baking sheet to drain.

Arugula Salad In a large bowl, toss together the arugula, lemon juice, salt, and pepper until the arugula is evenly coated.

To serve In the center of each of 4 dinner plates, spoon a little of the creamy goat cheese. Top each with a crisp tortilla disk, a little of the arugula salad, some of the lobster meat, another crisp tortilla disk, a drizzle of the creamy goat cheese, and a little more arugula salad. Top with lobster meat. Drizzle the lobster emulsion around the plates, and if desired, dot with the Chive Oil.

CREAMY GOAT CHEESE

2 ounces soft goat cheese

¼ cup half-and-half

¼ teaspoon Roasted Garlic Puree (see recipe, page 205)

1 teaspoon honey

¼ teaspoon salt

⅛ teaspoon freshly ground black pepper

LOBSTER EMULSION

4 cups Lobster Broth (see recipe, page 188)

½ fresh habanero chile, stemmed and seeded

¾ cup canola oil

1 tablespoon honey

2 teaspoons sherry-wine vinegar

CRISP TORTILLAS

Canola oil, for frying

8 flour tortillas (4 inch)

ARUGULA SALAD

1 small bunch arugula, washed and dried, tough stems removed

¾ teaspoon freshly squeezed lemon juice

¼ teaspoon salt

⅛ teaspoon freshly ground black pepper

2 cups lobster meat from Boiled Lobster (see recipe, page 188)

Chive Oil (optional; see recipe, page 190)

Terrina de Cangrejo

Avocado and Crabmeat Terrine

Makes 4 servings

AVOCADO

4 ripe Haas avocados
1 tablespoon freshly squeezed lime juice
½ teaspoon salt
⅛ teaspoon freshly ground black pepper

CRABMEAT

½ pound cooked lump crabmeat
1 small shallot, minced
1 tablespoon chopped fresh cilantro
2 teaspoons freshly squeezed lime juice
¼ teaspoon salt
⅛ teaspoon freshly ground black pepper

MIZUNA

2 cups mizuna, washed and dried
½ teaspoon freshly squeezed lime juice
¼ teaspoon salt
⅛ teaspoon freshly ground black pepper

GARNISH

1 tablespoon white sesame seeds
Habanero–Red Bell Pepper Reduction (see recipe, page 189)
Chive Oil (optional; see recipe, page 190)

Crabmeat and avocado are a wonderful combination. I use it in my Gazpacho de Aguacate (see recipe, page 54). In this dish, the ingredients are stacked in a tower, and the mizuna, which has a pleasant bitterness similar to that of mustard greens, adds a sharpness. The sweet-hotness of the red pepper reduction is a nice counterpoint to the richness of the avocado.

Avocado Halve the avocados lengthwise. Remove the pits. With a spoon, scoop out the flesh. Place the flesh in a medium bowl. Season with the lime juice, salt, and pepper. Mash until the texture is chunky.

Crabmeat Place the crabmeat in a small bowl and season with the shallot, cilantro, lime juice, salt, and pepper.

Mizuna Place the mizuna in large bowl and season with lime juice, salt, and pepper.

To serve To form the terrine, use a 3- to 3½-inch ring mold, biscuit cutter, or cookie cutter with high sides. Or, form each terrine free-form. For each terrine, layer as follows: one-eighth of the avocado mixture, 2 tablespoons crabmeat, ¼ cup mizuna, another eighth of the avocado, and 2 tablespoons crabmeat. Carefully remove the mold if using. Top with mizuna.

Garnish each plate with white sesame seeds, Habanero–Red Bell Pepper Reduction, and a few drops of the Chive Oil, if desired.

Tartar de Atún

Tuna Tartare with Huitlacoche Vinaigrette and Blue Corn Tortilla Chips

Makes 4 servings

¾ pound very fresh tuna steak
¼ cup diced, seeded ripe tomato
3 tablespoons chopped white Spanish onion
1 tablespoon sherry-wine vinegar
1 teaspoon honey
¼ teaspoon salt
⅛ teaspoon freshly ground black pepper
½ cup canola oil
1 can (3.5 ounces) huitlacoche
1 tablespoon chopped fresh cilantro

GARNISH (optional)
Blue Corn Tortilla Chips (see recipe, page 204)
Guajillo Chile Oil (see recipe, page 190)

Huitlacoche (below), often called corn mushroom, is an edible fungus that grows naturally on the kernels of fresh corn during the rainy season. Silvery gray on the outside and black on the inside, huitlacoche lends a distinctive but elusive flavor wherever it is used in cooking.

This is a delicious and an unusual way of preparing fresh tuna. The huitlacoche adds an earthy, subtle taste. Serve the tartare as a first course or as a salad course by adding a little arugula or mixed greens.

Remove any skin and bones from the tuna. Cut into ¼-inch dice. In a nonreactive bowl, mix together the tuna, tomato, and onion.

In a small bowl, stir together the vinegar, honey, salt, and pepper. Slowly whisk in the oil until well blended. In another small bowl, mash the huitlacoche with a fork until smooth. Stir into the oil mixture along with the cilantro. Add to the tuna mixture and gently fold together with a rubber spatula to evenly coat all the ingredients. Refrigerate, covered, until the tartare is well chilled, about 1 hour.

To serve Divide the tartare among 4 plates, arranging in a cylinder in the center of the plate. If desired, insert 2 tortilla chips into each cylinder and decorate the plates with a few drops of Guajillo Chile Oil.

Cangrejos al Chile Pasilla

Pan-Fried Soft-Shell Crabs with Fava Bean Puree and Pasilla Chile Emulsion

Makes 4 servings

Fava beans are quite popular in Mexico. In most cases they're used in their dried form for making soups, or sometimes they're fried and tossed in chile powder and served as a finger food alongside cocktails. I like them when they're fresh and still young on the vine. Their sweet taste makes them a perfect pairing with soft-shell crabs. Both are usually available in the markets at around the same time in the spring. To liven up the dish, I drizzle a Pasilla Chile Emulsion over the plate.

Fava **Bean Puree** Remove the fava beans from their pods. In a small saucepan of boiling water, blanch the beans for 3 minutes. Drain in a sieve and rinse under cold water to stop the cooking. With a small paring knife, split the skin and pop out the beans. You should have about 1 cup. In a small saucepan, combine the cream and the beans and simmer for about 8 minutes. Pour the mixture into a blender and puree. Pour back into the saucepan. Season the puree with the salt and white pepper, and keep warm.

Arugula Salad In a medium bowl, toss together the arugula, lime juice, salt, and pepper until the arugula is evenly coated.

Soft-Shell Crabs In a large skillet, heat the oil. Dredge the crabs on both sides with the corn flour. Add the crabs to the skillet, shell side down, and sauté for 3 minutes. Turn the crabs over and sauté for another 3 minutes, or until cooked through.

To serve In the center of each of 4 large dinner plates, spoon a quarter of the fava bean puree. Arrange a quarter of the arugula salad over the puree on each plate, and then top with a crab. If desired, drizzle the Pasilla Chile Emulsion and the Chive Oil over the plates.

FAVA BEAN PUREE
1 pound fresh fava beans, in their pods
1 cup heavy cream
¼ teaspoon salt
⅛ teaspoon freshly ground white pepper

ARUGULA SALAD
1 small bunch arugula, washed and dried, tough stems removed
1 to 2 teaspoons freshly squeezed lime juice
¼ teaspoon salt
⅛ teaspoon freshly ground black pepper

SOFT-SHELL CRABS
2 tablespoons canola oil
4 small soft-shell crabs, cleaned and trimmed
Corn flour, for dredging

GARNISH (optional)
Pasilla Chile Emulsion (see recipe, page 191)
Chive Oil (see recipe, page 190)

Callos de Hacha Tonali

Pan-Fried Scallops with Beet Puree, Frisée Salad, and
Red Bell Pepper–Coriander Seed Emulsion

Makes 4 servings

The contrasting colors of the beet puree and the red bell
pepper sauce strikingly offset the scallops.

Beet Puree Preheat the oven to 350°F. Place the beets on a baking sheet. Roast until knife-tender, about 1 hour. When the beets are cool enough to handle, peel and dice them. In a saucepan, combine the beets and the cream and simmer for 10 minutes. Strain the beets over a bowl, reserving the cooking liquid. Spoon the beets into a small food processor or blender. Add a little of the cooking liquid, and puree. With the motor running, slowly add enough of the remaining liquid until the puree is loose but still firm enough to hold its shape on a plate. Season with the salt and white pepper. Set aside.

Frisée Salad In a medium bowl, toss together the frisée, lime juice, salt, and pepper.

Scallops In a large skillet, heat the oil over medium-high heat. Season the scallops with the salt and white pepper. Add the scallops to the skillet and sear until lightly golden, 3 to 4 minutes total, turning the scallops over once.

To serve In the center of each of 4 dinner plates, spoon a quarter of the beet puree. Arrange 3 scallops around the puree, and top with the frisée salad. Decorate with the bell pepper emulsion, and the Chive Oil, if desired.

BEET PUREE

2 red beets (about ¾ pound), trimmed
   and scrubbed

2 cups heavy cream

¼ teaspoon salt

⅛ teaspoon freshly ground white pepper

FRISEE SALAD

1 bunch frisée, trimmed, rinsed, and dried

1 tablespoon freshly squeezed lime juice

¼ teaspoon salt

⅛ teaspoon freshly ground black pepper

SCALLOPS

1 tablespoon canola oil

12 large sea scallops (about ¾ pound),
   cleaned

½ teaspoon salt

⅛ teaspoon freshly ground white pepper

¾ cup Red Bell Pepper–Coriander Seed
   Emuslion (see recipe, page 191)

Chive Oil (optional; see recipe, page 190)

Zihuatanejo Bay is a spectacular backdrop for the
dining room at La Casa que Canta (opposite page).

Terrina de Salmón Tartar

Salmon Tartare and Avocado Terrine with Jícama Salad and Pasilla Chile Oil

Makes 4 servings

JICAMA SALAD
½ small jícama, peeled and shredded (about 1 cup)
1 to 2 tablespoons Adobo (see recipe, page 192)
1 tablespoon chopped fresh cilantro
¼ teaspoon salt
⅛ teaspoon freshly ground black pepper

SALMON TARTARE
8 ounces fresh salmon fillet, cleaned and trimmed of all dark-colored fat, and diced
1 tablespoon freshly squeezed lemon juice
1 tablespoon snipped fresh chives
½ teaspoon salt
¼ teaspoon freshly ground black pepper

1 cup Guacamole (see recipe, page 202)

GARNISH (optional)
Chive Oil (see recipe, page 190)
Pasilla Chile Oil (see recipe, page 190)

The skin of the jícama (below) is easily peeled, revealing the sweet, crisp flesh that is ideally suited for salads.

Even though rare or uncooked salmon is usually bland tasting, you'll be surprised what a little avocado, jícama, and pasilla chile can do for the fish. This dish is best left to stand for about fifteen minutes before serving so the flavors can develop a bit.

Jícama Salad In a medium bowl, toss together the jícama, Adobo, cilantro, salt, and pepper until evenly coated.

Salmon Tartare In a nonreactive medium bowl, toss together the salmon, chives, lemon juice, salt, and pepper.

To serve In the center of each of 4 dinner plates, spread a ¼ cup of the jícama salad in a 3-inch circle. On top of that, spread a layer of ¼ cup of the Guacamole. Then top each with a ¼-cup mound of the salmon. Let the plates stand for about 15 minutes. If desired, garnish the plates with the Chive Oil and the Pasilla Chile Oil.

Pulpo en su Tinta

Octopus in Squid Ink with Sweet Potato Pancake and Pea Shoot Salad

Makes 4 servings

I first ate octopus while growing up in Acapulco, and it immediately became a favorite. Octopus is one of those ingredients that can be tricky to cook. Use baby octopus if available, since it is the most tender. Either cook pieces of the octopus very quickly, or simmer it for thirty to forty minutes. In this dish I simmer it, then dice it and sauté it quickly in squid ink. The ink is available in little packets and can be found in good-quality fish markets and grocery stores and in gourmet food shops. The Guajillo Chile Sauce in this dish is a pleasantly sharp accent to the richness of the octopus. Octopus also works well in ceviche, as in my Vuelve a la Vida (see recipe, page 37).

OCTOPUS
2 pounds baby octopuses, cleaned
1 tablespoon canola oil
1 tablespoon chopped white Spanish onion
2 teaspoons squid ink
¼ teaspoon salt
⅛ teaspoon freshly ground black pepper

PEA SHOOT SALAD
1 small bunch pea shoots, washed and dried
1 teaspoon freshly squeezed lemon juice
¼ teaspoon salt
⅛ teaspoon freshly ground black pepper

SWEET POTATO PANCAKES
1 medium sweet potato
1 cup heavy cream
¼ teaspoon salt
⅛ teaspoon freshly ground black pepper
2 large eggs
⅓ cup all-purpose flour
1 teaspoon snipped fresh chives
2 teaspoons butter

Guajillo Chile Sauce (see recipe, page 194)
Chive Oil (optional; see recipe, page 190)

ctopus In a large saucepan of simmering water, gently cook the octopuses until tender, 30 to 40 minutes. In a large bowl, combine water and ice. With a large slotted spoon, remove the octopuses from the water and plunge them into the ice water to stop the cooking. Remove from the ice water. Blot dry with paper towels. Slice the bodies into rings and coarsely chop the rest. Set aside while you prepare the salad and pancakes.

Pea Shoot Salad In a large bowl, toss together the pea shoots, lemon juice, salt, and pepper. Set aside.

Sweet Potato Pancakes Meanwhile, peel and dice the sweet potato. In a saucepan, simmer together the sweet potato, cream, salt, and pepper until the potato is tender, 15 to 20 minutes. Pour into a food processor. Blend until pureed. Scrape into a bowl. Stir in the eggs, flour, and chives. Let the batter stand for 5 minutes.

In a large skillet, heat the butter. Spoon ¼ cup batter for each pancake into the skillet. Cook for 2 to 3 minutes per side, or until golden brown. Keep warm. You will probably have some pancakes left over, since you only need 4. Wrap and refrigerate the extra for other meals.

Octopus In a large skillet, heat the oil. Add the onion and sauté until tender, for 2 to 3 minutes. Add the octopus, ink, salt, and pepper and sauté until heated through, 1 to 2 minutes.

To serve Onto each of 4 dinner plates, spoon about 3 tablespoons of the Guajillo Chile Sauce. Place a pancake in the center of each and spoon a quarter of the octopus mixture on top of each pancake. Arrange the pea shoot salad so it is sticking out of the top of the octopus mound. If desired, garnish the plate with the Chive Oil.

Quesadilla Abierta de Camarones

Open-Faced Shrimp Quesadilla with Cilantro Pesto and Arugula Salad

Makes 4 servings

Quesadillas are like little tortilla sandwiches that, depending on where you are in Mexico, can be stuffed with practically anything from zucchini blossoms (which I serve at the restaurant) to shark. With this in mind, I created my open-faced quesadilla. I use the flour tortilla as my canvas to hold all the different combinations I can possibly imagine. Here I combine shrimp with cilantro pesto and an arugula-avocado salad, but other times it may be a yellow mole with roast pork and apples, or a house-smoked salmon with roasted poblano chiles and goat cheese.

Adobo Shrimp Reserve ½ cup of the Adobo. In a medium bowl, toss together the shrimp and the remaining Adobo. Let marinate at room temperature for 30 minutes.

Tortilla Crisps Preheat the oven to 400°F. Cut the tortilla into 12 triangles and place on a baking sheet. Drizzle with the Cilantro Pesto and sprinkle with the cotija cheese. Bake until golden brown and crisp, 2 to 4 minutes. Remove the crisps to a wire rack.

Arugula Salad In a large bowl, toss together the arugula, avocado, lemon juice, salt, and pepper. Set aside.

To cook the shrimp In a large skillet, heat the oil over medium-high heat. Season the shrimp with salt. Add to the hot oil and cook until curled and opaque in the center, 3 to 4 minutes. Set aside.

Place the 4 flour tortillas on a baking sheet. Drizzle each tortilla with 2 tablespoons of the reserved Adobo. Sprinkle each with 2 tablespoons of the Oaxaca cheese. Bake the tortillas until the cheese melts, 1 to 2 minutes—the tortillas should not become crisp.

ADOBO SHRIMP

1 cup Adobo (see recipe, page 192)

12 jumbo shrimp (11 to 15 per pound), shelled and deveined

2 tablespoons canola oil

½ teaspoon salt

TORTILLA CRISPS

1 flour tortilla (12 inch)

¼ cup Cilantro Pesto (see recipe, page 197)

¼ cup grated cotija cheese or Parmesan cheese

ARUGULA SALAD

1 bunch arugula, washed and dried, tough stems removed

1 Haas avocado, halved, pitted, skin removed and flesh cut into cubes

2 teaspoons freshly squeezed lemon juice

¼ teaspoon salt

⅛ teaspoon freshly ground black pepper

4 flour tortillas (8 inch)

½ cup shredded Oaxaca cheese or mozzarella cheese

½ cup Cilantro Pesto (see recipe, page 197)

GARNISH (optional)

Grated cotija cheese or Parmesan cheese

Cilantro Pesto (see recipe, page 197)

Crema fresca or crème fraîche, stirred (or sour cream mixed with a little heavy cream)

To serve On each of 4 dinner plates, place a tortilla. Place a quarter of the salad in the center of each, and arrange 3 shrimp around the salad on each tortilla. Drizzle with the Cilantro Pesto and garnish each with 3 tortilla crisps. If desired, sprinkle the rims of the plates with the grated cotija cheese and drizzle with the Cilantro Pesto and the crema fresca.

Sopes Surtidos

Sopes with Rajas, Chicken Tinga, and Shredded Beef

Makes 8 servings (about 30 sopes)

SOPES

Double recipe of dough for Corn Tortillas
(see recipe page 204 and Note,
opposite page)

SHREDDED BEEF

6 ounces skirt steak

¼ white Spanish onion, cut into chunks

1 very small clove garlic, crushed

¼ teaspoon whole black peppercorns

1 small bay leaf

¼ teaspoon salt

1 cup Tomatillo Sauce (see recipe, page 196)

RAJAS

4 fresh poblano chiles

2 teaspoons canola oil

½ small white Spanish onion, chopped

¼ cup heavy cream

¼ teaspoon salt

⅛ teaspoon freshly ground black pepper

CHICKEN TINGA

1 boneless, skinless chicken breast half
(about 4 ounces)

2 teaspoons canola oil

½ small white Spanish onion, chopped

1 cup Sweet Chipotle Sauce (see recipe,
page 195)

¼ teaspoon salt

⅛ teaspoon freshly ground black pepper

1 cup Black Bean Puree (see Black Beans
recipe, page 186)

Canola oil, for frying

GARNISH (optional)

Grated cotija cheese or Parmesan Cheese

Tomatillo Sauce (see recipe, page 196)

Chopped fresh cilantro

Crema fresca or crème fraîche, stirred (or sour
cream mixed with a little heavy cream)

Sopes—little handheld tortillas—evoke memories of living in Mexico City as a teenager. I would often go out into the street looking for a quick snack and within a few steps, I'd usually find an older woman in a small stand, making these to order. I can still remember the great taste of fresh sopes, stuffed with black beans, crema fresca, and a green tomatillo salsa. The toppings are an ideal way to use leftovers at home—anything from black beans or cheese to shredded cooked chicken or beef.

Sopes Prepare the dough for corn tortillas. Pat into 30 (4-inch) tortillas, about ¼ inch thick. Cook according to directions (see page 204). When you remove a tortilla from the griddle, transfer it to a clean kitchen cloth, and, using the cloth and your fingers, pinch up the edge all around to from a ½-inch-high rim. Set the tortillas aside, covered.

Shredded Beef In a large saucepan, mix together the steak, onion, garlic, peppercorns, bay leaf, and salt. Add enough water to cover the ingredients. Bring to a boil, then lower the heat and simmer for 45 minutes or until the steak is tender. Remove the steak and let cool. (Save the broth for soups.) With a knife, shred the beef. In a saucepan, heat the Tomatillo Sauce. Add the shredded beef and set aside.

Rajas Preheat the grill or broiler. Grill or broil the chiles about 4 inches from the heat, turning occasionally, until evenly charred on all sides, 10 to 15 minutes. Place in a paper bag, seal, and let stand until cool enough to handle and the skin is loosened, about 10 minutes. Remove the chiles from the bag. Cut the chiles in half, remove the stems and seeds, and peel off the skins. Cut lengthwise into thin julienne strips. In a medium skillet, heat the oil over medium heat. Add the onion and sauté until softened, 4 to 6 minutes. Add the chile strips and the cream, and simmer until thickened, about 2 minutes. Season with the salt and pepper, and set aside.

Chicken Tinga In a large saucepan, combine the chicken breast with enough cold water to cover. Simmer until cooked through, about 10 minutes. Remove the chicken and let cool. With a knife, shred the chicken. In a large skillet, heat the oil over medium heat. And the onion and sauté until golden brown, about 6 minutes. Add the Sweet Chipotle Sauce, salt, pepper, and chicken, and set aside.

To serve Gently reheat the shredded beef, rajas, chicken tinga, and Black Bean Puree. In a large skillet, heat 1 tablespoon of the oil. Working in batches, add the sopes (or tortillas if using store-bought) and fry until crisp, about 1 minute, turning over once. With a slotted spoon, remove the sopes to a paper towel–lined baking sheet. Add more oil to the skillet as needed. Spread each sope with about 1 tablespoon of the Black Bean Puree, and then one of the three toppings: the chicken, beef, or rajas. Arrange 3 sopes on a plate. If desired, garnish with the cheese, Tomatillo Sauce, cilantro, and crema fresca.

Note You can substitute store-bought 4-inch corn tortillas for the homemade. You will probably need to trim the tortillas.

Carnitas de Pato

Duck Carnitas with Sweet Tomatillo Sauce and Grilled Pineapple

Makes 4 servings

Carnitas is a dish that originated in Michoacán in the Bajío region of Mexico. They usually begin with pork that is half boiled and half fried, resulting in a savory, moist meat, with a temptingly crisp outside. Served with guacamole and freshly made tortillas, carnitas is a popular dish for Sunday family get-togethers. But since I wanted to try a recipe that would use something other than pork, it occurred to me that duck was an excellent alternative. I could cook it in its own fat, as the French often do.

Duck Carnitas Preheat the oven to 350°F. In a large saucepan, heat the fat over medium heat until it liquefies. Place the duck legs in a deep roasting pan and pour the fat over the top—the legs should be covered. Cover the pan with aluminum foil and roast for 3 hours.

Carefully remove the duck legs from the fat. When cool enough to handle, remove the skin and bones and discard. Shred the duck meat—you should have about 2 cups. Season the meat with the salt and pepper.

In the 350°F. oven, heat the tortilla triangles on a baking sheet.

To serve In a small bowl, combine the onion and cilantro. On each of 4 dinner plates, place 3 tortilla triangles. Top each triangle with the onion-cilantro mixture, pineapple, and Sweet Tomatillo Sauce. If desired, decorate the plate with the Chive Oil and sprinkle each plate with about ⅛ teaspoon black sesame seeds. Pile the shredded duck in the center of each plate (reheat the duck in a skillet if necessary).

DUCK CARNITAS

2 quarts (8 cups) Duck Fat (see recipe, page 187) or purchased duck fat or lard

4 duck legs

½ teaspoon salt

¼ teaspoon freshly ground black pepper

2 flour tortillas (8 inch), each cut into 6 equal wedges

GARNISH

2 tablespoons chopped white Spanish onion

1 tablespoon chopped fresh cilantro

1 cup diced, grilled fresh pineapple (about five ¼-inch-thick slices)

1 cup Sweet Tomatillo Sauce (see recipe, page 196)

Chive Oil (optional; see recipe, page 190)

½ teaspoon black sesame seeds (optional)

Pechuga de Pato en Mole de Tamarindo

Pan-Seared Duck Breast with Tamarind Mole

Makes 4 servings

Duck is not widely eaten in Mexico, but I can think of no better way to serve it than with a mole. If you're not a fan of duck, you can easily substitute boneless, skinless chicken breasts. The pleasingly sour taste of the tamarind makes this mole unusual.

TAMARIND MOLE

2 teaspoons tamarind paste (see Note, opposite page)

¾ cup Chicken Stock (see recipe, page 186) or canned chicken broth

¼ cup Mole Poblano (see recipe, page 199)

1 to 2 teaspoons honey, depending on the sweetness of the mole

1 teaspoon sherry-wine vinegar

¼ teaspoon salt

⅛ teaspoon freshly ground black pepper

SWEET POTATO PUREE

1 medium sweet potato, peeled and cut into ¼-inch dice

1 cup heavy cream

¼ teaspoon salt

⅛ teaspoon freshly ground black pepper

DUCK BREASTS

2 teaspoons canola oil

4 skinless, boneless duck breast halves

½ teaspoon salt

¼ teaspoon freshly ground black pepper

ARUGULA SALAD

1 small bunch arugula, cleaned and stemmed

2 teaspoons freshly squeezed lemon juice

¼ teaspoon salt

CRISP SWEET POTATO CURLS

Canola oil, for frying

½ sweet potato, peeled

GARNISH (optional)

White sesame seeds

Chive Oil (see recipe, page 190)

The pulp of the tamarind pods (opposite page; see also page 27) can be processed into a paste that is used in cooking to add a slightly acidic, sour note.

Tamarind Mole In a small bowl, mash together the tamarind paste and ¼ cup of the Chicken Stock. Strain through a medium-mesh sieve placed over a small bowl, pushing on the solids with the back of a ladle or a rubber spatula to extract as much liquid as possible. Discard the solids in the sieve. In a medium saucepan, combine the tamarind liquid, the remaining stock, the Mole Poblano, honey, vinegar, salt, and pepper. Bring to a boil, then lower the heat and gently boil, uncovered, until thick enough to form a pool on a plate, about 10 minutes. Strain through a medium-mesh sieve over a medium bowl, pressing through with the back of a ladle or a rubber spatula. Adjust the taste with honey, vinegar, and salt and pepper, if needed. Keep warm in a small saucepan.

Sweet Potato Puree In a medium saucepan, combine the sweet potato and cream, and gently boil until tender, about 30 minutes. Pour into a blender and puree. Scrape into a saucepan. Season with the salt and pepper, and keep warm.

Duck Breasts In a large skillet, heat the oil over medium-high heat. Season the duck breasts with the salt and pepper. Add to the skillet and sear until cooked through and the skin is golden and crisp, about 2 minutes on each side. Let rest for 5 minutes, then cut diagonally across the grain into thin slices.

Arugula Salad Meanwhile, in a large bowl, toss together the arugula, lemon juice, and salt.

Crisp Sweet Potato Curls Heat 2 inches of oil in a deep saucepan over medium-high heat until it registers about 365°F. on a deep-fat frying thermometer. Using a vegetable peeler, peel thin shavings of the sweet potato. Working in batches, slip the shavings into the hot oil and fry until crisp, 30 to 45 seconds. Remove with a slotted spoon and transfer to a paper towel–lined baking sheet.

To serve In the center of each of 4 dinner plates, spoon a mountain of the sweet potato puree. Arrange the slices of duck upright against the side of the puree, and place a portion of the arugula salad on top. Spoon the mole around the bottom of the duck slices. Top the salad with a scattering of the sweet potato curls, and if desired, garnish the mole with the sesame seeds and decorate the plate with dots of the Chive Oil.

Note You can substitute 2 teaspoons tamarind concentrate for the paste. Mix the concentrate into the ¾ cup stock.

Chile en Nogada

Veal-Stuffed Poblano Chile with Walnut-Almond Sauce

Makes 4 servings

Pomegranates come into season during the late fall, and when that happened while I was a kid, there was fierce competition among my friends' mothers to see who could make the best stuffed chiles. The winner was usually my grandmother. I ate a lot of these then, but I didn't complain. The stuffed chile was, and still is, one of my favorite meals.

The three colors of the dish represent the Mexican flag—the green of the chiles, the white of the sauce, and the red of the pomegranate seeds. Originally created by nuns for a special occasion, the stuffed chiles were first served in a convent in Puebla in central Mexico, where pre-Columbian, Mexican, and colonial Spanish cultures have blended to create a vibrant cuisine.

Nogada Sauce Place the walnuts and almonds in a blender. Pulse to finely grind. Add the cinnamon, nutmeg, and salt. Add ¼ cup of the milk and blend to puree. Add the remaining milk and blend until very smooth. Transfer to an airtight container and place in the refrigerator. The sauce is served chilled.

Chiles Preheat the broiler. Place the whole chiles on a broiler-pan rack. Broil about 4 inches from the heat, turning the chiles over occasionally, until evenly blackened on all sides, 15 to 20 minutes. Place the chiles in a paper or plastic bag and seal. Let stand until cool enough to handle and the skins have loosened, about 15 minutes. Remove the skins. Cut a slit from the top of each chile down the side. Remove the seeds and veins. Set aside.

Stuffing In a large skillet, heat the oil over medium heat. Add the onion and sauté until softened, about 5 minutes. For the last 2 minutes, add the garlic. Add the veal and salt, and sauté, breaking up the meat with a wooden spoon, until no longer pink, about 8 minutes. Add the tomatoes, raisins, almonds, and pine nuts. Cook over medium heat until cooked

NOGADA SAUCE

1¼ cups walnuts (about 5 ounces)
⅓ cup blanched sliced almonds (about 1 ounce)
¼ teaspoon ground cinnamon
Pinch ground nutmeg
¼ teaspoon salt
1 cup milk

CHILES

4 fresh large poblano chiles

STUFFING

1 tablespoon canola oil
1 white Spanish onion, chopped
2 cloves garlic, chopped
1 pound ground veal
¼ teaspoon salt
1 pound tomatoes, peeled, halved, seeded, and cut into ½-inch cubes
½ cup dark seedless raisins
⅓ cup blanched sliced almonds (about 1 ounce)
3 tablespoons pine nuts (about 1 ounce)

GARNISH

Pomegranate seeds
Pomegranate Juice Reduction (see recipe, page 189)
Chive Oil (optional; see recipe, page 190)

through and most of the liquid has evaporated, about 20 minutes. Spoon the stuffing into the chiles, dividing equally.

To serve In the center of each of 4 large salad plates, spoon a little of the nogada sauce. Place a stuffed chile in the center of each, and spoon more sauce over the chiles. Garnish with pomegranate seeds, drizzle with the Pomegranate Reduction, and dot with the Chive Oil, if desired. Serve at room temperature.

Tacos al Pastor

Tortillas with Grilled Adobo Pork and Pineapple

Makes 4 servings

PORK

1 cup Adobo (see recipe, page 192)

¼ cup orange juice

1 tablespoon sherry-wine vinegar

2 teaspoons honey

¼ teaspoon salt

⅛ teaspoon freshly ground black pepper

1 pork tenderloin (about 1¼ pounds), fat trimmed and sheath removed

GARNISH

1 teaspoon canola oil

1 cup diced fresh pineapple

1 cup diced white Spanish onion

1 tablespoon chopped fresh cilantro

1 tablespoon freshly squeezed lemon juice

16 Corn Tortillas (4 inch; see recipe, page 204), warmed, or store-bought corn tortillas, heated following package directions

Lime wedges

Chive Oil (optional; see recipe, page 190)

When it comes to tacos, this is one of my favorites, and perhaps the most popular pork taco in Mexico. What I like is the balance of flavors: the spiciness of the pork marinated in adobo and the sweetness of the pineapple quickly cooked with onion and then flavored with cilantro and lemon juice. All this is then wrapped in a fresh, handmade tortilla, still warm from the griddle. As if this weren't enough to get my mouth watering, I sometimes spoon on a little green tomatillo sauce (see recipe, page 196).

Pork In a glass baking dish, mix together ½ cup of the Adobo, the orange juice, vinegar, honey, salt, and pepper. Add the pork loin and turn to coat. Cover and refrigerate for 2 hours to marinate, turning the pork occasionally.

Preheat the grill or broiler. Remove the pork from the marinade and discard the marinade. Grill or broil the pork about 6 inches from the heat, turning occasionally, until cooked through, about 25 minutes. Let stand for about 5 minutes, then cut into small dice. In a medium saucepan, combine the pork and just enough Adobo to moisten the pork. Keep warm over low heat.

Garnish In a small skillet, heat the oil over medium heat. Add the pineapple and onion and sauté until slightly softened, about 6 minutes. Stir in the cilantro and lemon juice.

To serve On each plate, place 4 tortillas. Top each with the pork mixture and then the pineapple mixture. Place lime wedges on the plates and, if desired, drizzle the Chive Oil over the tacos.

Quesadillas Surtidas

Zucchini and Poblano Chile Quesadillas

Makes 4 servings

ZUCCHINI STUFFING

1 tablespoon canola oil

½ white Spanish onion, sliced

2 cloves garlic, minced

1 zucchini, trimmed, cut into thin julienne

½ teaspoon salt

⅛ teaspoon freshly ground black pepper

POBLANO CHILE STUFFING

1 fresh poblano chile

1 tablespoon canola oil

½ white Spanish onion, sliced

2 cloves garlic, minced

2 tablespoons heavy cream

¼ teaspoon salt

⅛ teaspoon freshly ground black pepper

8 Corn Tortillas (6 inch; see recipe, page 204)
    or store-bought corn tortillas

1 cup shredded Oaxaca cheese or
    mozzarella cheese

Canola oil, for frying

1 cup Black Bean Puree (see Black Beans
    recipe, page 186), warmed

GARNISH (optional)

Tomatillo Sauce (see recipe, page 196)

Spicy Tomato Sauce (see recipe, page 195)

Crema fresca or crème fraîche, stirred
    (or sour cream mixed with a little
    heavy cream)

Grated cotija cheese or Parmesan cheese

You can find quesadillas at street stands throughout Mexico, but to this day, when I think of quesadillas I remember those of my grandmother's cook, Catlina—they were the best. The deep-fried quesadillas in this recipe are similar to Catlina's.

Zucchini Stuffing In a large skillet, heat the oil over medium heat. Add the onion and sauté over medium heat until softened, about 6 minutes, without allowing the onion to brown. Add more oil as needed to prevent sticking. For the last 2 minutes of cooking, add the garlic. Add the zucchini and sauté until softened and it has released most of its liquid, 6 to 8 minutes. Season with the salt and pepper, and set aside.

Poblano Chile Stuffing Preheat the broiler. Broil the chile about 4 inches from the heat, turning often, until evenly charred on all sides, 5 to 10 minutes. Place the chile in a paper bag, seal, and let stand until cool enough to handle, about 10 minutes. Remove from the bag and peel off the skin. Halve the chile lengthwise and remove the stem and seeds. Cut the chile lengthwise into thin julienne. In a medium skillet, heat the oil over medium heat. Add the onion and sauté until softened, about 6 minutes, without letting the onion brown. For the last 2 minutes of cooking, add the garlic. Then add the chile, cream, salt, and pepper. Simmer for 30 to 60 seconds, or until the cream is absorbed. Set aside.

Off center on one tortilla, spoon 2 tablespoons of the Oaxca cheese, leaving a border around the edge. Spoon 2 tablespoons of the zucchini stuffing on top of the cheese. Fold the tortilla over and press the edges together. (If using store-bought tortillas, first heat in a dry skillet to make pliable. Then fill and fold over, wet the edges with a little water, and press the edges together. They will not seal as well as fresh tortillas.) Repeat with 3 more tortillas. Place on a jelly-roll pan lined with a damp kitchen towel. Repeat with the remaining 4 tortillas, using 2 tablespoons cheese and 2 tablespoons poblano chile stuffing per tortilla. Cover the quesadillas with plastic wrap and refrigerate.

In a large saucepan, heat about 3 inches of oil until it registers 350°F. on a deep-fat frying thermometer. Working in batches to avoid crowding the pan, add the quesadillas.

Fry until golden brown and slightly crisp, 1 to 2 minutes per side. With a slotted spoon, remove the quesadillas to a paper towel–lined baking sheet to drain.

To serve In the center of each of 4 large dinner plates, spoon ¼ cup of the Black Bean Puree. Arrange 2 differently filled quesadillas on each plate. If desired, decorate with the Tomatillo Sauce, Spicy Tomato Sauce, crema fresca, and cotija cheese.

Queso Fundido con Champiñones Adobados

Melted Manchego Cheese with Adobo Mushrooms and Tomatillo Sauce

Makes 4 servings

You might describe this cheese dish as the Mexican version of chips and dip. The toppings can range from chorizo to wild mushrooms, and the accompaniments are often corn or flour tortillas and a green or red salsa.

Mushrooms Adobados In a large skillet, heat the oil. Working in two batches if necessary, add the mushrooms to the skillet and sauté until softened and the liquid has been released, 6 to 8 minutes. Add the Adobo and cilantro and season with the salt and pepper. Cook until thickened, about another 3 minutes. Set aside.

Queso Fundido In a medium saucepan, melt the cheese over low heat, tossing with tongs as it becomes stringy, 3 to 4 minutes.

To serve Pour the cheese into a serving bowl or crock. If needed, rewarm the mushrooms. Spoon the mushrooms over the cheese in the bowl, and serve with the Tomatillo Sauce and warm Corn Tortillas.

MUSHROOMS ADOBADOS

1 tablespoon canola oil

½ pound shiitake mushrooms, cleaned, tough stems removed, caps sliced

½ pound cremini mushrooms, cleaned, tough stems removed, caps sliced

½ pound portobello mushrooms, cleaned, tough stems removed, caps sliced

½ cup Adobo (see recipe, page 192)

1 tablespoon chopped fresh cilantro

½ teaspoon salt

⅛ teaspoon freshly ground black pepper

QUESO FUNDIDO

12 ounces soft manchego cheese (not aged), grated

ACCOMPANIMENTS

½ cup Tomatillo Sauce (see recipe, page 196)

8 Corn Tortillas (6 inch; see recipe, page 204), warmed, or store-bought corn tortillas, heated following package directions, or flour tortillas

Salmón Maya

Pan-Roasted Salmon with Chayote Gratin and Potato Crisp

Makes 4 servings

Chayote is somewhat bland tasting, with a watery texture similar to that of a jícama or a radish. In this recipe, I bake slices of the chayote in a casserole-like dish with heavy cream and goat cheese, and then layer a portion of the gratin between the Black Bean Stock Reduction and the salmon— it acts as a flavor bridge between the two. You can also serve the Chayote Gratin on its own as a rich vegetarian dish.

Salmon Preheat the oven to 350°F. Remove the skin and any small bones from the salmon. Cut the fillet crosswise into 4 equal strips, about 1 inch wide (see photos, page 115). Cut each strip in half lengthwise for a total of 8 long strips. Take 2 strips, and curve each into a C shape, with the skin side on the inside. Fit the two pieces together to form a ring or medallion, and with a piece of kitchen twine, tie the two pieces together. Repeat with the remaining 6 pieces of salmon to form a total of 4 medallions. Season with the salt and pepper. Set aside.

In a large ovenproof skillet, heat the butter over medium-high heat. Add the salmon medallions and sear until lightly browned on each side, about 4 minutes total. Place the skillet in the oven and bake until the salmon is cooked through, another 1 to 2 minutes.

To serve In the center of each of 4 large, shallow dinner plates, ladle ¼ cup of the Black Bean Stock Reduction. Place a portion of Chayote Gratin in the center of each, and then top with a Potato Crisp. Remove the string from the salmon medallions and place a medallion on top of each crisp. If desired, decorate the Black Bean Reduction with the Roasted Tomato Vinaigrette and the Chive Oil.

SALMON

1½ pounds salmon fillet, cut from the center section of the fillet

½ teaspoon salt

¼ teaspoon freshly ground black pepper

2 tablespoons unsalted butter

1 cup Black Bean Stock Reduction (see recipe, page 186)

Chayote Gratin (see recipe, page 206)

4 Potato Crisps (see recipe, page 206)

GARNISH (optional)

Roasted Tomato Vinaigrette (see recipe, page 202)

Chive Oil (see recipe, page 190)

(Pages 110 to 111, from left) A young boy waits patiently in the Mercado Libertad in Guadalajara. Red snapper is a popular fish in Mexico and is used in the famous dish pescado a la veracruzana. Mexico has a long tradition of arts and crafts, including stone carving, which is celebrated at Maya and pictured here at the Villa Montaña hotel in Morelia, Michoacán. Grapes are ready for harvesting in Valle de Guadalupe, Mexico's wine-growing region in Baja.

Salmón al Chipotle

Pan-Roasted Salmon with Rice Noodles and
Asparagus in Coconut-Chipotle Sauce

Makes 4 servings

COCONUT-CHIPOTLE SAUCE

1 or 2 canned chipotle chiles in adobo
1 can (14 ounces) unsweetened coconut milk
2 teaspoons freshly squeezed lemon juice
1 tablespoon honey, or to taste
¼ teaspoon salt
⅛ teaspoon freshly ground black pepper

1½ pounds salmon fillet, cut from the center
    section of the fillet
½ teaspoon salt
¼ teaspoon freshly ground black pepper

¼ pound rice noodles
1 cup 1-inch pieces asparagus (about 4
    ounces)
3 tablespoons unsalted butter
12 mussels, scrubbed and debearded
12 large shrimp (21 to 30 per pound), shelled
    and deveined, each cut crosswise into
    4 equal pieces
½ cup 1-inch scallion pieces (2 scallions)
½ cup peanuts, coarsely chopped
½ cup chopped fresh cilantro
Salt, to taste
Freshly ground black pepper, to taste

GARNISH (optional)

Chive Oil (see recipe, page 190)
Guajillo Chile Oil (see recipe, page 190)

Of all my dishes, this is probably the one that is the least Mexican. I enjoy going to Thai restaurants and ordering pad thai—it probably has something to do with my liking for chiles. Salmón al Chipotle is a version of that rice-noodle dish with shrimp, presented in a kind of Mexican way. In fact, in this recipe you can omit the salmon and still have a great noodle dish. Instead of using Thai bird chiles, this entrée gets its heat from chipotle chiles in adobo.

Coconut-Chipotle Sauce In a blender, combine the chiles and a little of the coconut milk. Blend until the chiles are pureed in the coconut milk. Combine with the remaining milk in a medium saucepan. Gently boil over medium-low heat until reduced to about 1 cup, about 20 minutes. Stir in the lemon juice, and then the honey, adjusting the amount according to the hotness of the chiles. Season with the salt and pepper.

Prepare the salmon (see photos, opposite page) Remove the skin and any small bones from the salmon. Cut the fillet crosswise into 4 equal strips, about 1 inch wide. Cut each strip in half lengthwise, for a total of 8 long strips. Take 2 strips, and curve each into a C shape with the skin side on the inside. Fit the two pieces together to form a wheel or medallion, and with a piece of kitchen twine tie the pieces together. Repeat with the remaining 6 pieces of salmon to form a total of 4 medallions. Season with the salt and pepper. Set aside.

Cook the noodles according to the package directions. Drain well.

In a large pot of boiling water, cook the asparagus until crisp-tender, 3 to 5 minutes. Drain and run under cold water to stop the cooking. Drain again.

In a large skillet, heat 1 tablespoon of the butter. Add the mussels and shrimp and ¼ cup

HOW TO FORM SALMON MEDALLIONS

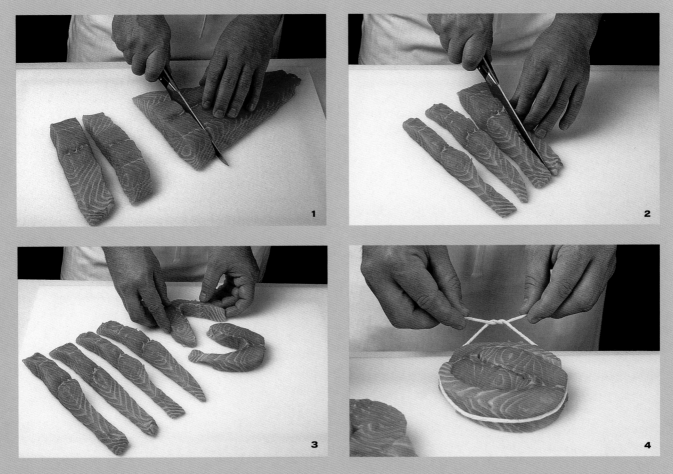

1 From the center section of the salmon fillet, cut 4 equal strips, about 1 inch wide. **2** Cut the pieces in half. **3** Take 2 strips of salmon and curve each into a C shape, with the skin side on the inside. Fit the 2 pieces snugly together. **4** Tie the pieces together around the circumference with a piece of kitchen twine to form a medallion.

coconut-chipotle sauce. Cover the skillet and cook, shaking the skillet occasionally, until the mussels open, 2 to 3 minutes. Add the noodles, asparagus, scallions, peanuts, and the remaining sauce, and cook over medium heat until the mixture is heated through. Add ½ to 1 cup water for a slightly soupy consistency. Stir in the cilantro, and season with salt and pepper. Remove from the heat.

Meanwhile, preheat the oven to 350°F. In a second, large ovenproof skillet, heat the remaining 2 tablespoons butter. Add the salmon medallions and sear until lightly browned on each side, about 4 minutes total. Place the skillet in the oven and bake until the salmon is cooked through, another 1 or 2 minutes.

To serve With tongs, remove the mussels from the noodle mixture. Into each of 4 large, shallow soup bowls, spoon a quarter of the noodle mixture. Snip the string from the salmon medallions, and place a salmon medallion on top of each pile of noodles. Arrange 3 mussels in each bowl, spoke-fashion. If desired, decorate the plate with the Chive Oil and the Guajillo Chile Oil.

Wine and Mexican Food

The Marriage

Wine brings joy and excitement to the dining experience, and its role in shaping a meal should be to complement—not complicate—the flavors of the food. When properly paired with food, wine is a meal's best friend.

To make good wine selections, it is important to understand the flavors and textures of the food being served. For example, the balance of spiciness and sweetness in some of my dishes calls for medium-bodied wines with good acidity and a bold fruit flavor. On the other hand, those dishes with heavy, intense flavors and textures work well with full-bodied, straightforward wines.

A dry white wine such as a **Sauvignon Blanc** matches perfectly with dishes that are acidic and spicy, such as ceviche. The Sauvignon Blancs that are crisp, lively, and slightly smoky are a good counterpoint to strongly flavored dishes such as Taco de Camarones seasoned with adobo (see recipe, page 81), and even a rich Guacamole (see recipe, page 202). Chile and New Zealand produce good Sauvignon Blancs, so make sure to sample them.

A **Chardonnay** that is full-bodied offers a balance of fruit, acidity, and texture, with hints of green apple, fig, and melon, as well as a little vanilla and oak. This wine complements dishes that often contain cheese or a creamy sauce, such as Langosta y Camarones with its rich corn puree (see recipe, page 140); Camarones al Chipotle in a smoky chile-cheese sauce (see recipe, page 134); and Ostiones Sandoval topped with two kinds of cheese and a creamy habanero chile rouille (see recipe, page 79). In other

words, match bold-flavored wines with rich foods. I like the Burgundian-style Chardonnays, such as the French Meursaults and Puligny-Montrachets, or those from California's Russian River and Carneros regions.

Chardonnays, however, should not be paired with food containing tomato or spicy chile broths. For these dishes and for something a little different, try an Albariño, an interesting varietal from Spain. It has high acidity with a slightly tart, clean, refreshing taste. Pair it with spicy fish dishes such Huachinango a la Talla with adobo and slices of tomato (see recipe, page 121), and Camarones Maya and its spicy tomato broth (see recipe, page 136).

Pinot Gris and **Pinot Grigio** are light, slightly sweet, aromatic whites that take the bite out of chiles—a touch of sweetness balances the heat.

Pinot Noir is often referred to as the perfect food wine. It's vibrant and fruity, and the delicate floral aroma and lingering rich flavor of black cherries complement many dishes. Grilled meats and fish have a tendency to become lightly caramelized with a slightly sweet flavor, so a Pinot Noir that is smooth with a touch of acidity is an excellent choice for those dishes. I also recommend Pinot Noir to accompany Tampiqueña, with its rich potato gratin (see recipe, page 159), and Pipian de Puerco, a tamarind-marinated pork loin (see recipe, page 155). Try the Pinots from California's central coast and Carneros regions.

Generally, foods with strong, heavy, intense flavors call for bold, robust, full-bodied wines such as **Cabernet Sauvignon, Syrah,** sometimes called, **Shiraz,** and **Zinfandel.** Steak and lamb dishes stand up to and tame the strong tannin of Cabernet Sauvignon. Syrah, a Rhône varietal with its dark berries and spice flavors, is perfect with all red meats, and in particular spicy dishes or ones infused with chiles. Stick with the Syrah of the Rhône or the Australian Cabernets, Shiraz, and blends of both varietals.

Zinfandels characteristically exhibit the flavor of fresh blackberries, with high levels of acidity, alcohol, and tannin. Old-vine Zinfandels with slightly lower acidity marry well with lamb dishes such as Cordero en Mole Verde (see recipe, page 165) and Mixiote de Cordero (see recipe, page 160).

Grapes have been cultivated in Valle de Guadalupe in Baja (opposite page) for several centuries. One of the major wineries is Monte Xanic (above).

Rioja, a blend of aromatic Tempranillo, Grenache, and often other varietals, is identified by its sweet, fragrant fruitiness with a high alcohol content. It's a fitting accompaniement to duck and lamb shank.

Mexican Wines

Although grapes have been in cultivation in Mexico for more than five hundred years, only recently has modern Mexican wine-making begun to develop. The primary wine-growing region is the Valle de Guadalupe, inland from Ensenada on the Baja peninsula and about an hour-and-a-half drive south of San Diego. Here the cool ocean breezes coupled with a small amount of rainfall during the winter months create conditions suitable for growing grapes. The major wineries in the region are Monte Xanic, Château Camou, L.A. Cetto, and Casa Pedro Domecq, and among them they produce Chardonnays, Sauvignon Blancs, Fumé Blancs, Cabernet Sauvignons, and Cabernet blends. An increasing number of small wineries are improving the quality of Mexican wines, as well.

Quesadilla Abierta de Salmón Ahumado

Open-Faced House-Smoked Salmon Quesadillas with Oaxaca Cheese

Makes 4 servings

½ cup hickory chips for barbecuing

SALAD

2 cups mixed baby lettuces, washed and dried

1 tablespoon freshly squeezed lemon juice

¼ teaspoon salt

⅛ teaspoon freshly ground black pepper

TORTILLAS

4 flour tortillas (8 inch)

½ cup shredded Oaxaca cheese or mozzarella

¼ cup crumbled fresh goat cheese

¾ pound salmon fillet, cut from the center section, skin and small bones removed

½ cup Chive-Habanero Rouille (optional; see recipe, page 201)

Workers in a tortilla factory in Guadalajara (opposite page) weigh and wrap flour tortillas in paper, getting them ready for shipment.

When I started to create open-faced quesadillas, instead of the classic deep-fried Mexican version (see Quesadillas Surtidas, page 108), I wanted to come up with a salad version that was on the lighter side. I liked the idea of using salmon and decided first to try smoking my own. The flavor turned out to be so good that I ended up using it in many other dishes, too. So, here's a hint: smoke a few extra pounds at a time so you have leftovers. I like to marinate pieces of smoked salmon fillet in an Adobo (see recipe, page 192) and then quickly grill it. Also, open-faced quesadillas don't necessarily have to be for dinner. If you use smaller tortillas, you can serve them as appetizers or snacks at a party.

In a large bowl of warm water, soak the hickory chips for at least 30 minutes. Drain the chips and pat dry with paper towels. Line a wok or large heavy skillet with aluminum foil. Scatter the chips over the bottom. Place a wire rack inside the wok over the chips. Place the wok, with its ring, over a burner. Tightly cover the wok and heat over medium-high heat until the chips begin to smoke, 5 to 10 minutes. Adjust the heat as needed.

Salad In a large bowl, toss together the lettuces, lemon juice, salt, and pepper. Set aside.

Tortillas On a baking sheet, place the tortillas in a single layer. Sprinkle each tortilla with the Oaxaca cheese and the goat cheese.

Preheat the broiler. Uncover the wok or skillet and place the salmon on the rack. Recover and smoke over medium heat for 3 to 5 minutes for a light smoky flavor. Carefully uncover the wok and transfer the salmon to a plate. Remove the wok from the heat, keeping covered.

Cut the salmon across the width into 4 equal pieces. Place, skinned side down, on a broiler-pan rack. Broil the salmon about 4 inches from the heat until just cooked through, 3 to 4 minutes. Place the baking sheet with the tortillas on a lower rack in the oven and heat just until the cheese melts, 1 to 2 minutes—do not allow the tortillas to become crisp.

To serve Place 1 tortilla on each of 4 dinner plates. Place the salad in the center of each tortilla and top with a piece of salmon. If desired, garnish with the Chive-Habanero Rouille.

Huachinango a la Talla

Pan-Roasted Adobo Red Snapper with Chipotle Coleslaw

Makes 4 servings

This could be the most famous fish dish in Acapulco. Tourists from all over the world visit Barra Vieja, a well-known beach where there are lots of outdoor cafés, and it is here that this dish became famous. Diners pick out their own whole fish, which is literally just hours out of the water. Then it is cleaned, seasoned, brushed with adobo, and grilled in an open pit—a simple dinner, served with tortillas. I've been there hundreds of times to savor this wonderful preparation. What follows is my version—the same adobo-flavored fish, but served on a bed of coleslaw tossed in a chipotle mayonnaise.

Season the fish with the salt and pepper. In a small bowl, stir together the Adobo and mayonnaise. Place the fish in a baking dish and coat with the Adobo mixture. Cover the dish with plastic wrap and refrigerate for 2 hours.

Chipotle Coleslaw In a large bowl, toss together the cabbages, cilantro, lemon juice, salt, and pepper. Stir in enough of the Chipotle Rouille to evenly moisten the coleslaw, ¼ to ½ cup. Add honey to taste, and stir to blend well.

Preheat the oven to 350°F. In a large, oven-proof skillet, heat 1 tablespoon of the oil. Add the fish and sear on both sides until lightly browned, 4 to 5 minutes total. Slide the skillet into the oven and bake until cooked through and the fish flakes when tested with a fork, another 4 to 5 minutes.

In a large skillet, heat the remaining 1 tablespoon oil. Add the tortilla halves and gently heat through, 1 to 2 minutes.

To serve In the center of each of 4 dinner plates, place a tortilla half. Layer the tomato slices on the tortilla. Spoon a quarter of the coleslaw on the tomatoes on each plate, and then top with a piece of red snapper. If desired, garnish the plate with more Chipotle Rouille and the Chive Oil.

1½ pounds red snapper fillet, cut from the center section, skin and any small bones removed, cut crosswise into 4 equal pieces

¼ teaspoon salt

⅛ teaspoon freshly ground black pepper

½ cup Adobo (see recipe, page 192)

½ cup mayonnaise

CHIPOTLE COLESLAW

2 cups shredded red cabbage

2 cups shredded Napa cabbage

½ cup chopped fresh cilantro

1 tablespoon freshly squeezed lemon juice

½ teaspoon salt

¼ teaspoon black pepper

Chipotle Rouille (see recipe, page 201)

Honey, to taste

2 tablespoons canola oil

2 Corn Tortillas (about 6 inch; see recipe, page 204), or store-bought tortillas, each cut in half

2 tomatoes, cored and cut into ¼-inch-thick slices

GARNISH (optional)

Chipotle Rouille (see recipe, page 201)

Chive Oil (see recipe, page 190)

In an updated version of pescado a la talla, the dish that Acapulco made famous, the fish is pan-seared (opposite page). But for the complete experience, people flock to the restaurants along the beach, including the Restaurante Tres Marias at Laguna de Coyuca (pages 122 to 123), to order a simple dinner of fish grilled over an open pit and served with homemade tortillas.

Huachinango Quetzal

Red Snapper with Cactus Salad and Black Bean and Red Pepper Sauces

Makes 4 servings

CACTUS SALAD

3 flat cactus paddles or leaves
    (about 8 x 4 inches)

2 tablespoons canola oil

½ cup chopped white Spanish onion

2 small tomatoes, chopped

¼ cup sherry-wine vinegar

¼ cup honey

1 tablespoon chopped fresh cilantro

¼ teaspoon salt

⅛ teaspoon freshly ground black pepper

BLACK BEAN SAUCE

1 cup Black Bean Puree (see Black Beans
    recipe, page 186)

2 teaspoons sherry-wine vinegar

2 teaspoons honey

Salt and freshly ground black pepper, to taste

CILANTRO SHRIMP (optional)

12 jumbo shrimp (11 to 15 per pound), peeled
    with tails intact, deveined

¼ cup canola oil

2 tablespoons chopped fresh cilantro

¼ teaspoon salt

⅛ teaspoon freshly ground black pepper

RED SNAPPER

1½ pounds red snapper fillet, cut from
    center section, skin and any
    small bones removed, cut crosswise
    into 4 equal pieces

¼ teaspoon salt

¼ teaspoon freshly ground black pepper

2 tablespoons butter

GARNISH (optional)

Roasted Red Bell Pepper Sauce (see recipe,
    page 196)

Tomatillo Sauce (see recipe, page 196)

Crisp Tortilla Strips (see recipe, page 204)

This dish is a winner in a couple of different ways. In 1991, I created it for a national chefs' contest in Mexico that is held annually to promote the culinary arts—and the fish won. After that, whenever I opened a restaurant I included the snapper on the menu, and it always seems to be a popular choice.

Cactus Salad Preheat the grill or broiler. Trim the edges from the cactus paddles. With a sharp knife, scrape or slice off the spiny bumps on both sides of the cactus paddles. Grill or broil the cactus paddles about 4 inches from the heat until soft and tender, about 4 minutes per side. Cut into ¼-inch squares. In a medium skillet, heat the oil. Add the onion and sauté until softened, about 6 minutes. Add the cactus and sauté for another 4 minutes. Remove the skillet from the heat. In a medium bowl, mix together the cactus mixture and tomatoes. In a small bowl, whisk together the vinegar, honey, cilantro, salt, and pepper. Add to the cactus mixture and toss to coat.

Black Bean Sauce In a small saucepan, combine the Black Bean Puree, vinegar, and honey. Season with salt and pepper, if needed. Gently heat, stirring occasionally, over low heat. Keep warm.

Cilantro Shrimp If making the shrimp, in a large bowl, mix together the shrimp, oil, cilantro, salt, and pepper. Cover and let stand at cool room temperature for 20 minutes.

Heat a large skillet over medium-high heat. Lift the shrimp from the marinade, add to the skillet, and sauté until they are curled and pink, 3 to 4 minutes.

Red Snapper Season each side of the pieces of fish with the salt and pepper. In a large skillet, heat the butter over medium-high heat. Add the fish and sauté until cooked through, about 4 minutes per side.

To serve In the center of each of 4 large dinner plates or shallow soup bowls, ladle about ¼ cup of the black bean sauce. Spoon about 1 cup of the cactus salad over the sauce on each plate. Top with a piece of red snapper. If using the shrimp, arrange 3 of them, spoke-fashion, on each plate and, if desired, decorate the plate with the Roasted Red Bell Pepper Sauce and the Tomatillo Sauce, and top the snapper with a pile of Crisp Tortilla Strips.

Huachinango Frito

Pan-Fried Red Snapper with Black Rice and Blood Orange–Chipotle Reduction

Makes 4 servings

I clearly remember when I was a little boy in Acapulco—my parents always ordered for me a fried fish that was served whole with rice and beans and fresh corn tortillas. Every time I return to Acapulco, I order that fried fish—it's simplicity at its best.

Marinated Onions In a medium bowl, stir together the onion, orange juice, lemon juice, honey, cilantro, salt, and pepper. Cover and let stand for 20 to 30 minutes.

Black Rice In a medium saucepan, heat the oil. Add the rice and sauté until lightly golden, about 3 minutes. Add the stock and season with the salt and pepper. Bring to a boil, stirring. Cover, reduce the heat, and simmer over low heat until the liquid is absorbed and the rice is tender, about 15 minutes. Drain off any excess liquid. Keep warm.

Red Snapper In a large skillet, heat the oil over medium-high heat. Season the fish fillets with salt and pepper. Add to the skillet and sear until cooked through, 3 to 4 minutes per side. If the portions are large, cut the fillets in half.

To serve In the center of each of 4 dinner plates, spoon a portion of the rice, about 1 cup. Place the fish on top of each. Garnish the fish with the onions. Spoon the Blood Orange–Chipotle Reduction on the plates around the rice, and if desired, garnish with orange zest and drops of Chive Oil.

MARINATED ONIONS

½ red onion, cut into thin julienne strips

1 tablespoon freshly squeezed orange juice

2 teaspoons freshly squeezed lemon juice

2 teaspoons honey

1 tablespoon chopped fresh cilantro

½ teaspoon salt

⅛ teaspoon freshly ground black pepper

BLACK RICE

1 tablespoon canola oil

1 cup uncooked long-grain white rice

3 cups Black Bean Stock (see Black Beans recipe, page 186)

½ teaspoon salt

⅛ teaspoon freshly ground black pepper

RED SNAPPER

2 teaspoons canola oil

4 red snapper fillets (about 5 ounces each), with skin

¼ teaspoon salt

⅛ teaspoon freshly ground black pepper

Blood Orange–Chipotle Reduction (see recipe, page 189)

GARNISH (optional)

Strips of orange zest

Chive Oil (see recipe, page 190)

Róbalo en Caldo de Cangrejo

Huazontle-Crusted Striped Bass in Spicy Crab Broth

Makes 4 servings

CRAB BROTH

1 tablespoon tomato paste

2 quarts water

2 carrots, trimmed and cut into chunks

½ white Spanish onion, cut into chunks

2 fresh serrano chiles, stemmed, seeded, and chopped

6 small live crabs, such as blue crabs

MUSHROOM DUMPLINGS

2 teaspoons canola oil

2 cups chopped wild mushrooms, such as shiitake or cremini (about 4 ounces)

¼ teaspoon salt

⅛ teaspoon freshly ground black pepper

8 wonton wrappers

STRIPED BASS

1¼ pounds striped bass fillet, cut from the center section, then cut crosswise into 4 equal pieces

¼ teaspoon salt

⅛ teaspoon freshly ground black pepper

1 bunch huazontle or broccoli rabe, rinsed, dried, and finely chopped

2 tablespoons canola oil

4 teaspoons freshly squeezed lemon juice

Epazote Oil or Chive Oil (optional; see recipe, page 190)

Several ships of the Mexican navy dock in the bay at Acapulco (opposite page).

Crab soup is a tasty and popular way to make use of the plentiful crabs in Mexico. From coast to coast, you'll find many variations, some spicier than others, some with fish, some with vegetables. My fish preparation here gains a fair amount of heat from the serrano chiles, and to make the dish even more souplike, you can break up the fish into small pieces and add some diced vegetables. Huazontle is a wild green with long, serrated leaves, and stalks with small seeds. Its flavor is similar to that of broccoli rabe, and, in fact, broccoli rabe is a good substitute.

Crab Broth In a small bowl, stir together the tomato paste and 1 to 2 tablespoons of the 2 quarts of water to dissolve the paste. In a large saucepan, combine the carrots, onion, chiles, dissolved tomato paste, and the remaining water. Bring to a boil. Add the crabs and cover the pan. Reduce the heat and simmer for about 50 minutes. Strain through a sieve over a large bowl, and discard the solids. Reserve the crab broth. (Save the crabs, if desired, for other uses, although the meat will be overcooked. When they are cool enough to handle, remove the meat from the legs, claws, and body.)

Mushroom Dumplings In a medium skillet, heat the oil over medium-high heat. Season the mushrooms with the salt and pepper. Add to the skillet and sauté until softened and most of the liquid has evaporated, 4 to 5 minutes. In the center of each of the wonton wrappers, spoon about 2 teaspoons of the cooked mushrooms. Moisten the edges of a wrapper, and fold it diagonally in half over the filling, pinching the edges together to seal. (Or bring the corners up and gently twist the top together to make a purse or little bundle.) Repeat with the remaining wrappers. In a saucepan, bring the crab broth to a simmer. Gently slip in the dumplings. Simmer until tender, 2 to 3 minutes. Remove the dumplings with a slotted spoon, transfer to paper towels, and gently blot dry. Keep warm in a 200°F. oven.

Striped Bass Season the bass fillets with the salt and pepper. Spread the huazontle on a piece of waxed paper. Place the fillet pieces on the waxed paper, skin side down. Sprinkle the huazontle over the pieces of fish to make a thick coating and gently press with your fingers to make it adhere to the fish. In a large skillet, heat the oil over medium-high heat. Add the fillets, coated side down, and sear until the coating is lightly browned, about 3 minutes. Turn the pieces over and continue to cook until the fish just flakes when tested with a fork, 3 to 4 minutes or longer, depending on the thickness of the fish.

To serve Spoon the crab broth among 4 shallow soup bowls. Drizzle each with 1 teaspoon lemon juice. Place a fillet in each bowl, coated side up, along with 2 dumplings. If desired, drizzle with the Epazote or Chive Oil.

Pescado al Chipotle

Pan-Seared Grouper with Huitlacoche Rice
and Mushroom-Chipotle Sauce

Makes 4 servings

Rice, just like beans, is a staple in Mexican cooking, and also like beans can be prepared in a variety of ways and served as an entrée, an accompaniment, or even as a garnish. At my grandmother's house in Mexico, rice was almost always part of the meal. One of the dishes that has stuck in my mind is rice mixed with huitlacoche, or corn fungus. I use it here as a "bed" for the fish.

MUSHROOM-CHIPOTLE SAUCE

2 teaspoons canola oil

1 cup chopped fresh wild mushrooms, such as shiitake or chanterelles (about 2 ounces)

1 small clove garlic, finely chopped

2 cups heavy cream

2 tablespoons Veal Stock (see recipe, page 187) or Chicken Stock (see recipe, page 186) or canned chicken broth

1 canned chipotle chile in adobo

2 teaspoons chopped fresh thyme

2 teaspoons chopped fresh cilantro

HUITLACOCHE RICE

3 tablespoons huitlacoche

1 tablespoon canola oil

1 tablespoon chopped white Spanish onion

1 cup uncooked long-grain white rice

3 cups Chicken Stock (see recipe, page 186) or canned chicken broth

1 teaspoon truffle oil (optional)

¼ teaspoon salt

⅛ teaspoon freshly ground black pepper

GROUPER

2 tablespoons canola oil

1¼ pounds grouper fillet, cut from the center section, skin and any small bones removed, cut crosswise into 4 equal pieces

½ teaspoon salt

¼ teaspoon freshly ground black pepper

Chive Oil (optional; see recipe, page 190)

Mushroom-Chipotle Sauce In a skillet, heat the oil. Add the mushrooms and garlic, and sauté until softened and most of the liquid is released, 3 to 5 minutes. Add the cream, stock, and chile, and simmer, uncovered, for 15 minutes, or until slightly thickened. Remove the chile and discard. Stir in the thyme and cilantro, and keep the sauce warm.

Huitlacoche Rice In a small bowl, stir and mash the huitlacoche with a fork. Set aside. In a medium saucepan, heat the oil over medium heat. Add the onion and sauté until softened, about 3 minutes. Add the rice and sauté until lightly colored, about 3 minutes. Add the stock, huitlacoche, truffle oil, if using, the salt, and pepper. Bring to a boil. Cover the pan, reduce the heat, and simmer until the rice is tender and the liquid has been absorbed, about 15 minutes. Drain any excess liquid.

Grouper In a large skillet, heat the oil. Season the grouper with the salt and pepper. Add the grouper to the skillet and sear until cooked through, about 3 minutes per side.

To serve In the center of each of 4 dinner plates, spoon about ¼ cup of the mushroom-chipotle sauce. Top each with a quarter of the rice, and then a piece of grouper. If desired, garnish with the Chive Oil.

Halibut con Pepitas

Pumpkin Seed–Crusted Halibut with Huitlacoche Mashed Potatoes, Caramelized Chayote, and Guajillo Chile Emulsion

Makes 4 servings

Coating the halibut with pumpkin seeds and then sautéing the fillets creates a pleasing crispness as well as a delicious nuttiness that goes well with the earthy flavor of the huitlacoche (pictured on pages 132 to 133).

Caramelized Chayote In a large skillet, heat the oil over medium heat. Add the chayote and sauté for 2 minutes. Stir in the honey and butter and sauté for 3 to 5 minutes, until the chayote is well coated and light golden. Season with the salt and pepper. Keep warm.

Halibut In a food processor, coarsely chop the pumpkin seeds. Season the halibut pieces with the salt and pepper. Coat the meaty side (the nonskin side) of the fillets with the pumpkin seeds. In a large skillet, heat the oil over medium heat. Add the fillets, pumpkin-seed side down, and sauté for 4 minutes, or until the pumpkin seeds are lightly colored. Turn the fillets over and sauté for another 5 minutes, or until cooked through.

To serve In the center of each of 4 large dinner plates, spoon a quarter of the Huitlacoche Mashed Potatoes. Place a piece of the halibut, pumpkin-seed side up, on each mound of potatoes. Spoon the chayote around the potatoes, and drizzle with the Guajillo Chile Emulsion. If desired, garnish with Chive Oil.

CARAMELIZED CHAYOTE

1 tablespoon canola oil

2 chayotes, peeled, halved, pitted, and cut into ¼-inch dice

2 tablespoons honey

1 tablespoon unsalted butter

¼ teaspoon salt

⅛ teaspoon freshly ground black pepper

HALIBUT

⅔ cup hulled, unsalted pumpkin seeds (about 4 ounces)

1¾ pounds halibut fillet, cut from the center section, skin and any small bones removed, cut crosswise into 4 equal pieces

¼ teaspoon salt

¼ teaspoon freshly ground black pepper

2 tablespoons canola oil

Huitlacoche Mashed Potatoes (see recipe, page 205)

Guajillo Chile Emulsion (see recipe, page 191)

Chive Oil (optional; see recipe, page 190)

Camarones al Chipotle

Shrimp with Chipotle Sauce, Black Bean Huarache, and Frisée Salad

Makes 4 servings

CHIPOTLE SAUCE WITH GOAT CHEESE

½ cup crema fresca or crème fraîche, stirred (or sour cream mixed with a little heavy cream)

½ cup chopped, seeded tomato

2 canned chipotle chiles in adobo

1 tablespoon chopped fresh cilantro

2 tablespoons soft goat cheese

¼ cup chopped white Spanish onion

1 to 2 tablespoons honey, or to taste

¼ teaspoon salt

⅛ teaspoon freshly ground black pepper

HUARACHES

Canola oil, for frying

8 Corn Tortillas (4 or 5 inch; see recipe, page 204) or store-bought corn tortillas

½ cup Black Beans (see recipe, page 186), pureed

½ cup shredded soft Gouda cheese

FRISEE SALAD

¼ pound frisée, trimmed and cleaned

2 teaspoons freshly squeezed lemon juice

¼ teaspoon salt

Pinch freshly ground black pepper

SHRIMP

2 tablespoons butter

1 teaspoon canola oil

20 jumbo shrimp (11 to 15 per pound), peeled with tails intact, deveined

½ teaspoon salt

¼ teaspoon freshly ground black pepper

2 tablespoons tequila

GARNISH (optional)

Chive Oil (see recipe, page 190)

Grated cotija cheese or Parmesan cheese

The flavorful play of shrimp with chipotle chiles appealed to me from the very first time I had it in a dish served at Pacos, my favorite seafood restaurant in Acapulco. Tortillas accompanied the shrimp so you could create your own tacos. Here I've reshaped the taco concept into a huarache, which is a black bean filling sandwiched between two corn tortillas and then deep-fried. If you reduce the number of shrimp per serving from five to three, as pictured here, the result is an excellent first course.

Chipotle Sauce with Goat Cheese In a food processor or blender, combine all the sauce ingredients. Blend until a smooth puree. Adjust the seasoning with the honey. Using the back of a ladle or a rubber spatula, force the sauce through a medium-mesh sieve placed over a bowl. Store, tightly covered, in the refrigerator for up to 3 days.

Huaraches In a large deep saucepan, heat 2 inches of canola oil over medium-high heat until it registers 365°F. on a deep-fat frying thermometer. In the center of each of 4 of the tortillas, spread 2 tablespoons black bean puree, and then top each with 2 tablespoons cheese. Cover each tortilla with another tortilla. Dampen the edges with water, and press the edges together to seal. (If using store-bought tortillas, first heat in a dry skillet to make pliable. The edges will not seal as well as fresh tortillas.) Working in batches, slowly slide the huarache into the hot oil. Fry until lightly colored and crisp, 2 to 3 minutes, turning over once. Remove to a paper towel–lined baking sheet and keep warm.

Frisée Salad Meanwhile, in a medium bowl, toss together the frisée, lemon juice, salt, and pepper. Set aside.

Shrimp Preheat the oven to 350°F. In a large ovenproof skillet, heat the butter and oil over medium heat. Season the shrimp with the

salt and pepper. Add the shrimp to the skillet. Carefully add the tequila. Tilt the skillet to ignite the tequila, and when the flames die out, stir in ¼ cup of the chipotle sauce. Place the skillet in the oven and bake until the shrimp are curled and cooked through, about 2 minutes. Be careful not to overcook the shrimp, which is easy to do.

To serve In the center of each of 4 dinner plates, ladle a quarter of the remaining chipotle sauce, warmed. Place a huarache in the center of the sauce on each plate. Arrange 5 shrimp, standing up, spoke-fashion, on each huarache. Top with the frisée salad. Decorate the plate with drops of Chive Oil and sprinkle with the cotija cheese, if using.

Camarones Maya

Shrimp in Spicy Tomato and Bell Pepper Broth with
Roasted Chile Stuffed with Goat Cheese

Makes 4 servings

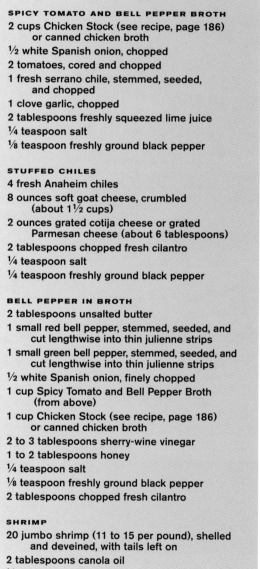

SPICY TOMATO AND BELL PEPPER BROTH
2 cups Chicken Stock (see recipe, page 186)
   or canned chicken broth
½ white Spanish onion, chopped
2 tomatoes, cored and chopped
1 fresh serrano chile, stemmed, seeded,
   and chopped
1 clove garlic, chopped
2 tablespoons freshly squeezed lime juice
¼ teaspoon salt
⅛ teaspoon freshly ground black pepper

STUFFED CHILES
4 fresh Anaheim chiles
8 ounces soft goat cheese, crumbled
   (about 1½ cups)
2 ounces grated cotija cheese or grated
   Parmesan cheese (about 6 tablespoons)
2 tablespoons chopped fresh cilantro
¼ teaspoon salt
¼ teaspoon freshly ground black pepper

BELL PEPPER IN BROTH
2 tablespoons unsalted butter
1 small red bell pepper, stemmed, seeded, and
   cut lengthwise into thin julienne strips
1 small green bell pepper, stemmed, seeded, and
   cut lengthwise into thin julienne strips
½ white Spanish onion, finely chopped
1 cup Spicy Tomato and Bell Pepper Broth
   (from above)
1 cup Chicken Stock (see recipe, page 186)
   or canned chicken broth
2 to 3 tablespoons sherry-wine vinegar
1 to 2 tablespoons honey
¼ teaspoon salt
⅛ teaspoon freshly ground black pepper
2 tablespoons chopped fresh cilantro

SHRIMP
20 jumbo shrimp (11 to 15 per pound), shelled
   and deveined, with tails left on
2 tablespoons canola oil
½ teaspoon salt
¼ teaspoon freshly ground black pepper

GARNISH (optional)
Roasted Red Bell Pepper Sauce (see recipe,
   page 196)
Chive Oil (see recipe, page 190)

(Opposite page) Richard Sandoval, Sous Chef Marcos,
and Grill Master Benancio work the stoves at Maya.

If you have visited any of the coastal cities of Mexico, you have probably tasted a dish similar to this one. It's a take on the traditional pescado a la veracruzana. Here I use shrimp rather than fish, but if you prefer, you can substitute pieces of red snapper.

Spicy Tomato and Bell Pepper Broth
In a small saucepan, combine the stock, onion, tomatoes, serrano chile, garlic, lime juice, salt, and pepper. Simmer for 20 minutes. Pour into a blender and puree. Reserve 1 cup for this recipe, and store the remainder, tightly covered, in the refrigerator for up to 1 week to use in soups and sauces.

Stuffed Chiles Preheat the broiler. Place the Anaheim chiles on a baking sheet and broil about 4 inches from the heat, turning the chiles over occasionally, until evenly blackened on all sides, 15 to 20 minutes. Place the chiles in a paper or plastic bag, and seal. Let stand until cool enough to handle and the skins have loosened, about 15 minutes. Peel off the skins. Cut a slit from the top of each down the side. Remove the stem, seeds, and veins, leaving the chiles whole. Set them aside.

Reduce the oven temperature to 350°F. In a small bowl, mash together with a fork the goat cheese, cotija, cilantro, salt, and pepper. Spoon into the 4 chiles, dividing equally. Place on a baking sheet and set aside.

Bell Pepper in Broth In a large skillet, heat the butter over medium heat. Add the bell pepper strips and sauté until slightly softened, about 4 minutes. Add the chopped onion, the reserved 1 cup spicy tomato broth, and the stock. Continue to cook over medium heat until the pepper is softened and the liquid is slightly reduced, 5 to 10 minutes. Season with the vinegar, honey, salt, and pepper, adjusting the vinegar and honey to taste, adding more if necessary. Stir in the chopped cilantro and keep warm.

Bake the stuffed chiles until heated through and the cheese is melted, 6 to 8 minutes. Remove from the oven and cover with foil to keep warm.

Shrimp Increase the oven temperature to broil. Rub the shrimp with the oil and season with the salt and pepper. Arrange on a broiler-pan rack and broil 4 to 6 inches from the heat until the shrimp are pink and curled and cooked through, turning occasionally, about 4 minutes—be careful not to overcook.

To serve In the center of each of 4 large, shallow soup bowls, using tongs, place a quarter of the bell peppers. Spoon the broth into the bowls around the peppers. Arrange 5 shrimp in each bowl around the peppers, and top the peppers with a stuffed chile. If desired, garnish the rim of the bowls with the Roasted Red Bell Pepper Sauce and Chive Oil.

Mariscada

Sautéed Scallops, Shrimp, Clams, and Mussels with Roasted Garlic Puree and Black Rice

Makes 4 servings

Mexico has an extensive coastline, bordered by the Gulf of California, the Pacific Ocean, the Gulf of Mexico, and the Caribbean. All of these waters provide the country with a great variety of seafood, and this main course takes advantage of that by combining many of those jewels of the sea on one plate. The rice is colored with black bean cooking liquid and flavored with fried plantains, and the sautéed seafood is seasoned with a robust garlic puree.

Black Rice In a medium skillet, heat 2 tablespoons of the butter over medium heat until bubbly. Add the plantain and sauté until light golden brown, about 3 minutes. Remove the plantain and set aside.

In a medium saucepan, heat the remaining 1 tablespoon butter over medium heat. Add the onion, cover the saucepan, and cook until softened, 4 to 6 minutes. Add the rice and cook, stirring, until lightly colored, about 2 minutes. Add the bean stock. Cover the saucepan and bring to a boil. Lower the heat and simmer, covered, until the rice is tender and the liquid is absorbed, about 15 minutes. Mix in the plantain and the salt and pepper.

Seafood Just before serving, in a large skillet, heat the butter over medium-high heat. Add the mussels, scallops, clams, and shrimp. Cover the skillet and cook, shaking the skillet occasionally, for 2 minutes or until the mussels and clams open. Uncover the skillet and sauté for another minute, or until everything is cooked through. Discard any shellfish that don't open. Stir in the Roasted Garlic Puree and season with the lemon juice, Maggi sauce, Tabasco sauce, salt, and pepper. Adjust the seasoning as needed.

BLACK RICE

3 tablespoons unsalted butter

1 yellow-black plantain, soft to the touch, peeled and cut into ¼-inch dice

½ cup chopped white Spanish onion

1 cup uncooked long-grain white rice

3 cups Black Bean Stock (see Black Beans recipe, page 186) or water

¼ teaspoon salt

⅛ teaspoon freshly ground black pepper

SEAFOOD

2 tablespoons unsalted butter

12 mussels in the shell, scrubbed and debearded

12 sea scallops

8 small clams in the shell, scrubbed

8 large shrimp (21 to 30 per pound), shelled and deveined but with tails intact

Roasted Garlic Puree (see recipe, page 205)

1 tablespoon freshly squeezed lemon juice

2 teaspoons bottled Maggi sauce

1 teaspoon Tabasco sauce, or to taste

¼ teaspoon salt

⅛ teaspoon freshly ground black pepper

GARNISH (optional)

Red Bell Pepper–Coriander Seed Emulsion (see recipe, page 191)

Chive Oil (see recipe, page 190)

To serve In the center of each of 4 large dinner plates or in 4 bowls, spoon about ¾ cup of the rice. On each plate, arrange 3 mussels, 3 scallops, 2 clams, and 2 shrimp. If desired, garnish with the Red Bell Pepper–Coriander Seed Emulsion and the Chive Oil.

Langosta y Camarones

Lobster and Shrimp with Roasted Corn Puree,
Watercress Salad, and Chive-Habanero Rouille

Makes 4 servings

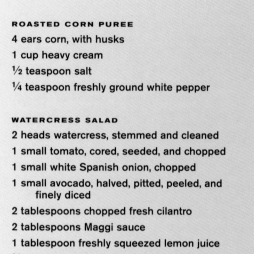

ROASTED CORN PUREE

4 ears corn, with husks

1 cup heavy cream

½ teaspoon salt

¼ teaspoon freshly ground white pepper

WATERCRESS SALAD

2 heads watercress, stemmed and cleaned

1 small tomato, cored, seeded, and chopped

1 small white Spanish onion, chopped

1 small avocado, halved, pitted, peeled, and
finely diced

2 tablespoons chopped fresh cilantro

2 tablespoons Maggi sauce

1 tablespoon freshly squeezed lemon juice

½ teaspoon salt

¼ teaspoon freshly ground black pepper

SEAFOOD

2 tablespoons canola oil

12 jumbo shrimp (11 to 15 per pound),
shelled and deveined but with tails intact

2 small lobsters (about 1½ pounds each),
cooked (see Boiled Lobster, page 188),
meat removed from shell (about
2 cups meat total)

½ teaspoon salt

¼ teaspoon freshly ground black pepper

Chile de Arbol–Tomato Seed Vinaigrette (see
recipe, page 200)

Chive-Habanero Rouille (see recipe,
page 201)

In this dish, I start with a rich, roasted corn puree foundation, and then lay on a lemony watercress salad and chunks of sweet lobster meat.

Roasted Corn Puree Preheat the broiler or grill. Broil or grill the corn in the husks about 6 inches from the heat, turning occasionally, until the husks are charred and the kernels are browned, about 20 minutes. When cool enough to handle, remove the husks and silk. Holding the ears upright, remove the kernels by slicing downward with a sharp knife against the cob. In a medium saucepan, combine the kernels and the cream, and season with the salt and white pepper. Simmer until the corn is tender, about 15 minutes. Pour the mixture into a blender and puree. Scrape into a saucepan and keep warm.

Watercress Salad In a large bowl, gently toss together the watercress, tomato, onion, avocado, and cilantro. In a small bowl, stir together the Maggi sauce, lemon juice, salt, and pepper. Add the dressing to the watercress mixture and toss to combine.

Seafood In a large skillet, heat the oil over medium-high heat. Season the shrimp and lobster with the salt and pepper. Add the shrimp to the skillet and sauté until almost cooked through, about 2 minutes. Add the lobster and cook another minute or so to heat through.

To serve In the center of each of 4 dinner plates, spoon a quarter of the roasted corn puree. Top with the watercress salad and a portion of the lobster meat. Drizzle each salad evenly with a little of the Chile de Arbol–Tomato Seed Vinaigrette. Arrange 3 of the shrimp around the salad on each plate. Garnish with the Chive-Habanero Rouille.

Cangrejos en Caldo de Frijol

Soft-Shell Crabs with Roasted Corn–Frisée Salad and Black Bean Broth

Makes 4 servings

Soft-shell crabs are not very popular in Mexico, but I love them. In New York City it's one of the expected rites of spring—diners search for them on menus as soon as they come into season. Every year I look forward to the day when my fish supplier tells me they have arrived. In Mexico, we usually use crabs to make broth (see Róbalo en Caldo de Cangrejo, page 128). So not surprisingly, I usually serve soft-shell crabs in a broth—here it's a black bean broth.

Roasted Corn–Frisée Salad Preheat the broiler or grill. Broil or grill the corn in the husks about 6 inches from the heat, turning occasionally, until the husks are charred and the kernels are browned in spots, about 20 minutes. When cool enough to handle, remove the husks and silk. Holding the ears upright, remove the kernels by slicing downward with a sharp knife against the cobs—you should have about 2 cups of kernels.

In a large skillet, heat the oil. Add the corn, onion, chile, ½ teaspoon of the salt, and ⅛ teaspoon of the pepper, and sauté until the corn and onion are softened, about 5 minutes. Stir in the bean stock and cilantro, and remove from the heat.

In a large bowl, toss together the frisée, lemon juice, and the remaining salt and pepper.

Soft-Shell Crabs In a large skillet, heat the oil. Dredge the crabs on both sides with corn flour. Add the crabs to the skillet, shell side down, and sauté for 3 minutes. Turn the crabs over and sauté another 3 minutes, or until cooked through.

To serve In the center of each of 4 dinner bowls, pile a quarter of the frisée. Top with a quarter of the corn-stock mixture and 2 crabs.

ROASTED CORN–FRISEE SALAD
4 ears corn, with husks

2 tablespoons canola oil

½ cup chopped white Spanish onion

1 fresh serrano chile, stemmed, seeded, and chopped

¾ teaspoon salt

¼ teaspoon freshly ground black pepper

1 cup Black Bean Stock (see Black Beans recipe, page 186)

¼ cup chopped fresh cilantro

1 head frisée lettuce, washed and dried

1 tablespoon freshly squeezed lemon juice

SOFT-SHELL CRABS
2 tablespoons canola oil

8 soft-shell crabs, cleaned and trimmed

Corn flour, for dredging

Moles

Mole excites the flavor of Mexican cooking as curry does with Thai and Indian cuisines. It would be impossible to say how many different versions of mole sauce there are, and each home cook always seems to throw in his or her own secret ingredient. But make no mistake, when you encounter the real thing, the taste is beyond words. The balance of chiles, sweet spices, onion, as well as other flavors make the sauce truly memorable. As far as I am concerned, it is one of a handful of classic sauces from around the world. If you don't have the dried chiles on hand, there are prepared versions of mole that make for an easy shortcut (see Mole, Notes on Ingredients, page 26).

Pechuga con Mole Poblano

Grilled Chicken Breast with Mole Poblano, Cilantro Rice, and Plantains

Makes 4 servings

One of my favorite moles includes chocolate—it's a classic. The sauce can be made ahead and refrigerated.

If desired, in a dry skillet toast the sesame seeds over medium heat, stirring, for about 1 minute—be careful, since some of the seeds will pop. Transfer the seeds to a plate to cool.

Cilantro Rice In a medium saucepan, heat the butter over medium heat. Stir in the onion, cover the saucepan, and cook or sweat the onion until softened, 3 to 4 minutes. Stir in the rice and cook, stirring constantly, until translucent, about 2 minutes. Add the stock, salt, and pepper. Bring to a boil. Lower the heat, cover, and cook until the liquid is absorbed and the rice is tender, 15 to 20 minutes. When cooked, stir in the cilantro.

Chicken Meanwhile, season the chicken breasts with the salt and pepper. In a large skillet, heat the oil. Add the chicken and sauté until cooked through, 2 to 3 minutes per side. Remove from the heat and keep warm.

Plantains In a large skillet, heat 2 tablespoons of the butter. Add 6 of the plantain slices and cook until golden brown and tender, about 2 minutes per side. Remove and keep warm. Repeat with the remaining butter and plantain slices.

To serve Slice the chicken breasts crosswise diagonally into thin strips. In the center of each of 4 dinner plates, spoon a mound of rice. Arrange the chicken breast slices on top of the rice. On each plate, arrange 3 plantain slices spoke-fashion against the rice to form a pyramid. Spoon the mole sauce on the plate and garnish, if desired, with the sesame seeds.

GARNISH (optional)
¼ cup sesame seeds

CILANTRO RICE
2 tablespoons butter
¼ cup chopped white Spanish onion
1 cup uncooked long-grain white rice
2 cups Chicken Stock (see recipe, page 186) or canned chicken broth
½ teaspoon salt
⅛ teaspoon freshly ground black pepper
½ cup chopped fresh cilantro

CHICKEN
4 boneless, skinless chicken breast halves (about 1 pound total)
½ teaspoon salt
¼ teaspoon freshly ground black pepper
2 tablespoons canola oil

PLANTAINS
4 tablespoons unsalted butter
2 yellow-black plantains, soft to the touch, peeled and each cut lengthwise into 6 long pieces

1 cup Mole Poblano (see recipe, page 199)

Chilaquiles

Grilled Chicken with Tortillas and Tomatillo Sauce

Makes 4 servings

CHIPS
Canola oil, for frying

10 white corn tortillas (6 inch)

Salt, to taste

CHICKEN
2 chicken breast halves on the bone, with skin (about 1¼ pounds total), bone removed

Olive oil, for brushing

½ teaspoon salt

¼ teaspoon freshly ground black pepper

2 cups Tomatillo Sauce (see recipe, page 196)

½ cup heavy cream

2 teaspoons honey, or to taste

¼ teaspoon salt

⅛ teaspoon freshly ground black pepper

1 cup Black Bean Puree (see Black Beans recipe, page 186), warmed

GARNISH
½ cup shredded soft manchego cheese

Crema fresca or crème fraîche, stirred (or sour cream mixed with a little heavy cream) (optional)

Grated cotija cheese or Parmesan cheese (optional)

I've often thought this dish was created to rescue all the leftover tortillas in the world. Whenever I make it, I think of Juanita and her husband, the couple who used to take care of my grandmother's house in Acapulco. I visited them frequently when I was a boy, and Juanita always had a treat for me. But what really remains vividly in my memory are the rows of tortillas lying out in the sun to dry for the chilaquiles that she would make the next morning for breakfast.

Chips In a large saucepan, heat 2 inches of canola oil until it registers 350°F. on a deep-fat frying thermometer. Cut each tortilla into 6 equal wedges. Working in batches, fry the tortilla pieces until crisp and golden brown, turning occasionally, 1½ to 2 minutes. With a slotted spoon, transfer the chips to a paper towel–lined baking sheet to drain.

Chicken Preheat the grill or broiler. Brush the chicken with the oil and season with the salt and pepper. Grill or broil the chicken about 6 inches from the heat, skin side facing heat, until browned, about 10 minutes. Turn over and continue to cook until cooked through, another 15 to 20 minutes. Let stand for about 10 minutes.

Meanwhile, in a large saucepan, bring the Tomatillo Sauce to a simmer. Stir in the heavy cream and honey, and season with the salt and pepper. Keep warm.

To serve Cut the chicken breasts crosswise on the diagonal into thin slices. Add the chips to the tomatillo sauce mixture in the saucepan and gently toss to coat. In the center of each of 4 large dinner plates, spread ¼ cup of the Black Bean Puree. Top with the coated chips, and arrange the chicken on top of the chips. Garnish with the manchego cheese. If desired, drizzle the plates with the crema fresca and sprinkle with the cotija cheese.

Pechuga Adobada

Adobo Chicken Breast with Roasted Corn, Pico de Gallo,
and Huitlacoche Dumpling

Makes 4 servings

ADOBO CHICKEN

4 boneless, skinless chicken breast halves
(about 5 ounces each), flattened

¼ teaspoon salt

⅛ teaspoon freshly ground black pepper

½ cup Adobo (see recipe, page 192)

PICO DE GALLO

2 large tomatoes, cored, seeded, and diced
(1½ cups)

¼ cup chopped white Spanish onion

1 fresh serrano chile, stemmed, seeded, and
chopped

1 tablespoon chopped fresh cilantro

2 teaspoons freshly squeezed lemon juice

1 teaspoon honey

½ teaspoon salt

¼ teaspoon freshly ground black pepper

ROASTED CORN

2 ears corn, with husks

1 tablespoon butter

¼ cup chopped white Spanish onion

½ teaspoon salt

¼ teaspoon freshly ground black pepper

1 tablespoon chopped fresh cilantro

HUITLACOCHE DUMPLINGS

¼ cup shredded Gouda cheese

4 teaspoons huitlacoche

4 wonton wrappers (3½ x 3 inches)

Canola oil, for frying

GARNISH

Cilantro Pesto (see recipe, page 197)

¼ cup toasted unsalted peanuts, ground

Grated cotija cheese or Parmesan cheese

Pico de gallo is to Mexicans what ketchup is to people in the United States. It's a wonderful sauce with tomatoes and fresh chiles that can be made in minutes, and it's delicious with anything from a plain piece of cooked chicken to a quesadilla—or as my wife, Gabriela, likes it, just by itself.

Adobo Chicken Season the chicken breasts with the salt and pepper. Brush with the Adobo. Refrigerate, covered, for 1 hour.

Pico de Gallo In a medium bowl, combine the tomato, onion, chile, and cilantro. In a small bowl, stir together the lemon juice, honey, salt, and pepper. Add to the tomato mixture and toss to combine. Let stand, covered, while preparing the rest of the recipe.

Roasted Corn Preheat the broiler or grill. Broil or grill the corn in the husks about 6 inches from the heat, turning occasionally, until the husks are charred and the kernels are browned, about 20 minutes. When cool enough to handle, remove the husks and silk. Holding the ears upright, remove the kernels by slicing downward with a sharp knife against the cobs.

In a large skillet, heat the butter. Add the onion. Season with the salt and pepper, and sauté until softened, about 4 minutes. Add the corn kernels and heat through, adding more butter if needed. Stir in the cilantro and remove from the heat.

Huitlacoche Dumplings In a small bowl, stir together the Gouda cheese and the huitlacoche. In the center of each of the wonton wrappers, place a heaping tablespoon of the cheese mixture. Lightly moisten the edges of the wrappers with water and fold diagonally in half, pressing the edges together to seal. If you like, form a bundle by bringing the corners up and over the top and twisting them

together. In a large, deep saucepan, heat about 2 inches of the oil until it registers 365°F. on a deep-fat frying thermometer. Working in batches if necessary, slip in the dumplings and fry until golden brown and crisp, 2 to 2½ minutes. With a slotted spoon, remove the dumplings to a paper towel–lined baking sheet.

Meanwhile, preheat the broiler or grill. Broil or grill the chicken breasts about 4 inches from the heat until cooked through, about 2 minutes per side. Cut across the grain into thin slices. Gently reheat the corn kernels.

To serve In the center of each of 4 dinner plates, spoon a quarter of the roasted corn. Pile the chicken on top, dividing equally among the plates. Garnish with the pico de gallo and the Cilantro Pesto. Sprinkle with the peanuts and the cotija. Top each with a dumpling.

Pozole de Pato

Pozole with Duck and Shredded Cabbage

Makes 4 servings

There are probably as many different versions of pozole—a hearty stew that originated in Guadalajara—as there are cooks who make it. Traditionally, in Acapulco every Thursday restaurants served pozole for lunch. My family would gather at one of the numerous spots throughout the city, and while the food was delicious, the lunch was really just an excuse for a weekly social event. My version is made with hominy—dried corn kernels—in a guajillo chile broth, and garnished with a mixture of shredded cabbage and radish, seasoned with cilantro and lemon juice. The dish usually includes braised pork or chicken, but here I use rich, flavorful duck.

Pozole In a large saucepan, heat 1 tablespoon of the oil. Add the onion and garlic, and sauté over medium-high heat until softened, about 4 minutes. Add the chiles and sauté until slightly darkened, 30 to 45 seconds per side. Add 2 cups of the stock and simmer until the chiles are softened, about 5 minutes.

Meanwhile, in a large skillet, heat the remaining 2 tablespoons oil. Add half of the hominy and sauté until crisp, about 5 minutes.

Pour the chile mixture into a blender and puree. Strain through a medium-mesh sieve back into the saucepan, pressing on the solids with the back of a ladle or a rubber spatula. Discard the solids in the sieve. Add all the hominy to the saucepan along with the bay leaf and the remaining stock. Bring to a boil. Lower the heat and simmer the pozole, partially covered, for 1 hour.

Cabbage Salad While the pozole is simmering, mix together the cabbage, radish, cilantro, lemon juice, salt, and pepper. Set aside.

Toward the end of the simmering time for the pozole, heat a large skillet over medium-high heat. Add the duck breasts, skin side down, and sear until crisp, about 5 minutes. Turn over and sauté until cooked through, 5 to 10 minutes. Transfer the duck to a cutting board and let

POZOLE
3 tablespoons canola oil
½ cup chopped white Spanish onion
2 cloves garlic, chopped
2 dried guajillo chiles, stemmed and seeded
4 cups Duck Stock (see recipe, page 187)
2 cups canned white hominy, drained
1 bay leaf

CABBAGE SALAD
1 cup shredded green cabbage
¼ cup shredded red radish (about 4 radishes)
1 tablespoon chopped fresh cilantro
2 teaspoons freshly squeezed lemon juice
¼ teaspoon salt
⅛ teaspoon freshly ground black pepper

4 boneless duck breast halves, with skin
1 tablespoon honey

GARNISH (optional)
Sliced radish
Chile powder

rest for 10 minutes, then slice each breast diagonally across the grain into 3 thin slices.

Season the pozole with the honey and salt and pepper, as needed.

To serve Among 4 shallow soup bowls, divide the pozole. Spoon ¼ cup of the cabbage salad in the center of the soup, and in each bowl arrange 3 pieces of duck breast upright around the cabbage. If desired, garnish with the radish and sprinkle the rim of the plate with the chile powder.

Chuleta de Puerco en Vinagre Balsamico

Pork Chop Stuffed with Chorizo and Apples
in Balsamic Vinegar–Adobo Sauce, with Garlic Mashed Potatoes

Makes 4 servings

Garlic Mashed Potatoes (see recipe,
    page 204)

CHORIZO AND APPLE STUFFING

1 chorizo sausage (about 6 ounces), cut into
    ¼-inch dice

1 small Granny Smith apple, peeled, halved,
    cored, and cut into ¼-inch dice

⅛ teaspoon freshly ground white pepper

PORK CHOPS

4 pork chops, about 1 inch thick
    (8 to 10 ounces each)

½ teaspoon salt

¼ teaspoon freshly ground black pepper

2 tablespoons canola oil

Balsamic Vinegar–Adobo Sauce (see recipe,
    page 188)

GARNISH (optional)

Green grapes, halved

Chive Oil (see recipe, page 190)

Stuffing the pork chops with diced apples and chorizo helps to keep the meat moist during the cooking. The creamy garlic mashed potatoes are perfect for soaking up the balsamic vinegar sauce.

Prepare the Garlic Mashed Potatoes and keep warm in a 200°F oven.

Chorizo and Apple Stuffing Heat a medium skillet over medium-high heat. Add the chorizo and sauté until darkened, about 6 minutes. Add the apple and sauté until slightly softened, 2 to 3 minutes. Season with the white pepper and set aside.

Pork Chops Preheat the oven to 400°F. Cut a horizontal pocket into the side of each pork chop without piercing the other side. Season with the salt and pepper. Spoon the stuffing into the chops. In a large skillet, heat the oil. Add the pork chops and sear until browned on both sides, 2 to 3 minutes per side. Place the chops in a baking dish and bake 16 minutes, turning the chops over halfway through.

To serve In the center of each of 4 large dinner plates, spoon 2 tablespoons of the Balsamic Vinegar–Adobo Sauce. Spoon a quarter of the Garlic Mashed Potatoes in the sauce and top with a stuffed pork chop. If desired, garnish with the grapes and drops of Chive Oil.

Pipian de Puerco

Tamarind-Rubbed Pork Tenderloin with Roasted
Corn Puree and Pumpkin Seed Sauce

Makes 4 servings

Here's another dish that I have to thank Juanita for—she was the wonderful woman who took care of my grandmother's house in Acapulco. I think what made her pumpkin seed sauce special was the combination of toasted peanuts, pecans, and almonds. I never got the recipe for Juanita's pork dish, but my re-creation is pretty close.

Pork Season the pork with the salt and pepper. In a large plastic food-storage bag or glass baking dish, coat the pork with the Tamarind Vinaigrette. Let stand while preparing the rest of the recipe.

Roasted Corn Puree Preheat the broiler or grill. Broil or grill the corn in the husks about 6 inches from the heat, turning occasionally, until the husks are charred and the kernels are browned, about 20 minutes. When cool enough to handle, remove the husks and silk. Holding the ears upright, remove the kernels by slicing downward with a sharp knife against the cob. In a medium saucepan, combine the corn kernels and cream. Season with the salt and white pepper. Gently boil for 15 minutes or until the corn is very tender. Pour the mixture into a blender or food processor and puree. You should have about 2 cups puree.

In a small skillet, bring the Pipian Sauce to a gentle boil and continue to boil until slightly thickened but still runny, 5 to 10 minutes.

Preheat the broiler or grill. Remove the pork from the Tamarind Vinaigrette and discard the vinaigrette. Broil or grill the pork about 4 inches from the heat, turning occasionally, until cooked through, 20 to 25 minutes. Let the pork rest for 5 minutes. Slice the pork diagonally into 4 equal pieces, and then slice each piece diagonally into 2 smaller pieces. Keep warm.

Gently reheat the corn puree and the Pipian Sauce in 2 separate saucepans.

PORK
1 pork tenderloin (about 1¼ pounds)
½ teaspoon salt
¼ teaspoon freshly ground black pepper
Tamarind Vinaigrette (see recipe, page 201)

ROASTED CORN PUREE
6 ears corn, with husks
1 cup heavy cream
½ teaspoon salt
⅛ teaspoon freshly ground white pepper

1 cup Pipian Sauce (see recipe, page 200)

Ground, toasted, hulled pumpkin seeds
(optional)

Villa Montaña in Morelia (opposite page) is the perfect setting for one of my favorite dishes.

To serve In the center of each of 4 shallow soup bowls, spoon a quarter of the corn puree. Arrange 2 pieces of the pork in each bowl on top of the puree. Ladle about ¼ cup of the Pipian Sauce around the corn puree in each bowl. Sprinkle the rim of the bowl with ground toasted pumpkin seeds, if using.

Lomo de Cerdo en Salsa de Chipotle

Adobo Pork Loin with Chipotle Sauce and Purple Mashed Potatoes

Makes 4 servings

ROASTED YELLOW TOMATO AND CHIPOTLE SAUCE

2 yellow tomatoes

½ cup chopped white Spanish onion

1 small clove garlic, chopped

2 teaspoons canola oil

1 canned chipotle chile in adobo

2 cups Veal Stock (see recipe, page 187) or
   Chicken Stock (see recipe, page 186) or
   ½ cup canned chicken broth

1 to 2 teaspoons honey

¼ teaspoon salt

⅛ teaspoon freshly ground black pepper

1 teaspoon chopped fresh cilantro

PORK WITH ADOBO RUB

2 dried pasilla chiles

2 teaspoons brown sugar

1 cinnamon stick, broken into pieces

¼ teaspoon salt

⅛ teaspoon freshly ground black pepper

1 pork tenderloin (about 1¼ pounds)

PURPLE MASHED POTATOES

10 small purple potatoes (about 1 pound),
   peeled and diced

1 cup milk

2 teaspoons butter

½ teaspoon salt

¼ teaspoon freshly ground black pepper

FRIED ONION

Canola oil, for frying

1 large egg

½ cup all-purpose flour

1 onion, halved and cut crosswise into
   thin slices

Chive Oil (optional; see recipe, page 190)

Chiles are such an important ingredient in Mexican cooking that it makes sense to buy them in bulk, rather than two or three at a time (opposite page).

An adobo sauce is an outstanding marinade for meats. But you can also make a dry adobo rub that can be patted onto meats just before grilling or broiling. This particular rub was created by Chucho, the first chef I worked with after graduation from the Culinary Institute of America. For the mashed potatoes I use purple potatoes, which are often used in South American cooking, and especially in many Peruvian dishes. These potatoes are now widely available in supermarkets and green grocers.

Roasted **Yellow Tomato and Chipotle Sauce** Preheat the oven to 350°F. Core the tomatoes and cut into quarters. Spread on a baking pan. In a small bowl, mix the onion, garlic, and oil, and spread on the pan along with the chipotle chile. Roast for 30 minutes.

Meanwhile, if using homemade stock, gently boil it in a saucepan until reduced to ½ cup.

Transfer the roasted vegetables and chile to a blender and puree. Add the stock and blend. Pour into a saucepan and season with the honey, salt, and pepper. Stir in the cilantro.

Pork with Adobo Rub Preheat the grill or broiler. Remove the stems and seeds from the pasilla chiles, and break the chiles into small pieces. In a blender, combine the chiles, brown sugar, cinnamon, salt, and pepper. Blend until a powder. Pat the seasoning rub over the pork tenderloin. Grill or broil the pork about 4 inches from heat, turning occasionally, just until pink in the center, 20 to 25 minutes, depending on the thickness of the meat and the desired doneness. Let the pork rest for 5 minutes, and then cut diagonally into 16 slices. Keep warm.

Purple Mashed Potatoes Meanwhile, in a medium saucepan of boiling salted water, cook the potatoes until soft, about 15 minutes.

Drain. Transfer the potatoes to a bowl and mash with the milk and butter. Season with the salt and pepper. Keep warm.

Fried Onion In a deep heavy saucepan, heat 2 to 3 inches of oil until it registers 365°F. on a deep-fat frying thermometer. Place the egg in a medium bowl and lightly beat with a fork. Spread the flour on a piece of waxed paper. Using a fork, dip the pieces of onion into the egg, and then remove, letting the excess drip back into the bowl. Drop onion pieces into the

flour and turn to thoroughly coat. Slide the coated onion pieces into the hot oil and fry until golden and crisp, about 2 minutes. Using a slotted spoon, transfer the onion pieces to a paper towel–lined baking sheet to drain.

To serve On each of 4 dinner plates, spoon ¼ cup of the chipotle sauce. Spoon a quarter of the mashed potatoes into a mound on top of the sauce. Arrange 4 slices of the pork around the potatoes, and top with the fried onion. If desired, decorate the sauce with the Chive Oil.

Pirámide de Res

Grilled Skirt Steak with Grilled Onions, Black Bean Puree, and Chile de Arbol Sauce

Makes 4 servings

1 tablespoon canola oil

4 slices (¼ inch thick) white Spanish onion

1 tablespoon freshly squeezed lemon juice

2 teaspoons Maggi sauce

Salt, to taste

Freshly ground black pepper, to taste

4 slices (¼ inch thick) tomato

4 pieces skirt steak (4 ounces each), trimmed and pounded to a thickness of about ¼ inch

1 cup Black Bean Puree (see Black Beans recipe, page 186), warmed

1 cup Guacamole (see recipe, page 202)

1 cup Crisp Tortilla Strips (see recipe, page 204)

GARNISH (optional)

Chile de Arbol Sauce (see recipe, page 194)

Chive Oil (see recipe, page 190)

This dish comes from my original menu when I first opened Maya in New York City. Truthfully, I was scared about what people would think about this new Mexican cooking. To be safe, I made something that most people recognized, but that was still a bit creative—a dish similar to fajitas.

reheat the grill or broiler.

In a large skillet, heat the oil. Add the onion slices and sauté over medium heat until softened and lightly golden, 8 to 10 minutes. Season with the lemon juice, Maggi sauce, salt, and pepper, and set aside.

Season the tomato slices with salt and pepper. Grill or broil 4 inches from the heat until softened, about 2 minutes per side.

Season the steak with salt and pepper. Grill or broil 4 inches from the heat until desired doneness, 3 to 4 minutes per side for medium-rare. Let stand for 5 minutes, then cut across the grain into thin slices.

To serve In the center of each of 4 dinner plates, spoon ¼ cup of the Black Bean Puree. Place a tomato slice on top of each, followed by a slice of onion, and then a pile of the sliced steak. Spoon ¼ cup of the Guacamole over the meat. Stick Crisp Tortilla Strips in the top, and, if desired, drizzle the plate with the Chile de Arbol Sauce and the Chive Oil.

Tampiqueña

Grilled Filet Mignon with Potato and Rajas Gratin and Mole Cheese Enchilada

Makes 4 servings

This very popular beef dish, thought to have been invented in the 1940s in the kitchen of the Tampico Club in Mexico City, is served in fondas, the equivalent of a casual diner or coffee shop in the United States. The presentation is almost instantly recognizable: the beef tenderloin (traditionally skirt steak is used) is butterflied into a long rectangular strip and arranged on the plate. I serve mine with a mole sauce and a potato and poblano chile gratin that soaks up the delicious sauce.

Place the tenderloin pieces, with a long side facing you, on a cutting surface. To butterfly the meat, start at a short end with a sharp knife and make a horizontal cut about ¼ inch up from the bottom, through the meat to within ¼ inch from the opposite side. Open the meat like a book. Repeat the horizontal cutting through the thicker portion of the meat and open again like a book. Continue the butterflying until you have a long strip of meat about ¼ inch thick. Repeat with the other pieces of meat. If the thickness is uneven, place the strip between sheets of waxed paper and gently pound with a rolling pin or the bottom of a heavy skillet to an even thickness. Season with the salt and pepper. Rub with the oil and set aside.

Enchilada Preheat the oven to 350°F. Heat a large skillet over medium heat. Add the tortillas and heat until soft and pliable, about 30 seconds per side. Spoon ¼ cup of the cheese across each tortilla, slightly off center, leaving a border, and fold the tortilla over. Place on a baking sheet. Bake until the cheese melts, about 2 minutes.

Meanwhile, grill or sear the meat in a large, heavy skillet for about 1 minute per side for medium-rare, or longer for desired doneness.

4 thick pieces beef tenderloin (filet mignon), 3 inches wide (6 ounces each)

½ teaspoon salt

¼ teaspoon freshly ground black pepper

1 tablespoon canola oil

ENCHILADA

4 Corn Tortillas (6 inch; see recipe, page 204) or store-bought corn tortillas

1 cup shredded Oaxaca cheese or mozzarella cheese

Potato and Rajas Gratin (see recipe, page 206)

1 cup Mole Poblano (see recipe, page 199)

1 cup Guacamole (see recipe, page 202)

GARNISH (optional)

Grated cotija cheese or Parmesan cheese or crumbled feta cheese

Chive Oil (see recipe, page 190)

To serve In the center of each of 4 large dinner plates, place a small square of the Potato and Rajas Gratin. Place an enchilada on one side of the plate and spoon the Mole Poblano over it. Arrange the strip of beef on the plate along with the Guacamole. Garnish with the cotija cheese and Chive Oil, if desired.

Mixiote de Cordero

Lamb with Achiote and Vegetables in Banana Leaf

Makes 4 servings

2 tablespoons canola oil, or more as needed

8 baby gold beets, trimmed, scrubbed, and halved through the stem

16 baby carrots, trimmed and scrubbed

1 chayote, peeled, halved, pitted, and diced

1½ pounds lamb sirloin or boneless leg of lamb, cut into large chunks

½ teaspoon salt

Pinch freshly ground black pepper

4 squares (12 inch) banana leaves, avocado leaves, or aluminum foil

1 cup Achiote Sauce (see recipe, page 192)

Aluminum foil for outer wrappers

Mixiotes are little packets of meat that in central Mexico are cooked in barbecue pits. The paper-thin skin from the leaves of the maguey, or century, plant is used as the wrapper. In the absence of having the plant or an open barbecue pit, which is usually the case at home and even in a restaurant kitchen, I like to use banana leaves to make these little pockets of chile-seasoned lamb, and then bake them in the oven.

In a large skillet, heat 1 tablespoon oil over medium heat. Add the beets and sauté until tender, about 20 minutes. For the last 5 minutes of cooking, add the carrots. Transfer them to a plate.

In same skillet, sauté the chayote until tender, about 5 minutes, adding more oil as needed to prevent sticking. Remove to the plate with the other vegetables.

Season the lamb with salt and pepper. In a large skillet, heat 1 tablespoon oil over medium-high heat. Working in batches, if necessary to avoid crowding the skillet, add the lamb and sear until browned, 2 to 4 minutes per side. Transfer to a clean plate.

In the center of each of the banana leaves or foil squares, place the pieces of lamb. Arrange the vegetables around the lamb, dividing equally. Ladle about ¼ cup Achiote Sauce over each portion. Fold the sides of each leaf or foil over to enclose the filling and make a neat package. Wrap each package in foil and place on a baking sheet—if using the foil for the first wrapping for the packet, there is no need to wrap a second layer around it.

Preheat the oven to 400°F. Bake the foil packets for 10 minutes, or until heated through. Remove from the oven. Remove the outer foil and discard. Open each packet and place one on each of 4 dinner plates.

Rack de Cordero en Mole Blanco

Rack of Lamb with White Chocolate Mole and Potato Gratin

Makes 4 servings

FRISEE SALAD

1 small bunch frisée, cleaned, tough stems
   removed

2 teaspoons freshly squeezed lemon juice

½ teaspoon salt

⅛ teaspoon freshly ground black pepper

LAMB

1 whole rack of lamb (about 7½ pounds),
   trimmed, cleaned, and cut in half
   (see Note)

½ teaspoon salt

⅛ teaspoon freshly ground black pepper

2 tablespoons canola oil

Potato Gratin (see recipe, page 206)

Mole Blanco (see recipe, page 199)

Chive Oil (optional; see recipe, page 190)

One of my goals in cooking is to strive to keep all the flavors in balance, with no single note dominating. When I created this dish for my restaurant, I knew I wanted to serve a mole with the elegant rack of lamb entrée. But at the same time, I realized that the traditional, darker chocolate mole would probably overpower the delicate flavor of the lamb. So I experimented and came up with this more subtle white-chocolate mole.

Frisée Salad In a large bowl, toss together the frisée, lemon juice, salt, and pepper until the frisée salad is evenly coated.

Lamb Preheat the oven to 400°F. Season the lamb with the salt and pepper. In a large skillet, heat the oil over medium heat. Add the lamb and sear until browned, 6 to 8 minutes per side. Transfer the lamb to a roasting pan. Roast until medium-rare, 12 to 14 minutes. Let rest for 5 minutes, then cut the rack into individual chops.

To serve On each of 4 large dinner plates, place a portion of the Potato Gratin, and surround with 4 chops. Garnish with the frisée salad and the Mole Blanco, and, if desired, dot with the Chive Oil.

Note Have your butcher remove the cross bone along the bottom of the rack, so you can more easily divide the rack into individual chops after cooking. For a more elegant presentation, you can also ask the butcher to French the ribs, which means trimming and cleaning the rib bones.

Cordero en Mole de Pétalos de Rosa

Lamb with Rose Petal Mole

Makes 4 servings

After seeing the movie *Like Water for Chocolate*, I thought it only natural to create a rose petal mole and serve it at my restaurant. So I spent a few days experimenting with roses, rose tea, and finally rose water, and the rose water is finally what gave me the best results.

Pinto Bean Puree In a small food processor, puree together the pinto beans, cooking liquid, salt, and pepper. Transfer to a small saucepan and keep warm.

Baby Beets and Swiss Chard In a large skillet, heat the butter over medium heat. Add the beets and season with the salt and pepper. Sauté until slightly tender, about 5 minutes. Add the chard and continue to sauté until the beets are tender and the chard has cooked down, about 5 minutes. Add the vinegar and sauté for 1 minute. Keep warm.

Rose Petal Mole While the beets and chard are cooking, in a small saucepan, heat the Mole Poblano over medium heat, stirring. Stir in the honey to taste, balancing the spiciness of the mole. Stir in the rose water and keep the mole warm.

Lamb Preheat the grill or broiler. Rub the lamb with the oil, then season with the salt and pepper. Cook about 4 inches from the heat, for 3 to 4 minutes per side for medium rare. Cut each piece of lamb diagonally in half.

To serve In the center of each of 4 dinner plates, spoon about ¼ cup of the bean puree. Place a quarter of the chard on top of the puree, and 2 pieces of halved sirloin on top of that. On each plate, arrange 4 beets around the bean puree. Then spoon small pools of the mole on the plates and if desired, dot the plates with the Chive Oil.

PINTO BEAN PUREE

1 cup cooked dried pinto beans or 1 cup drained canned pinto beans

⅓ cup bean cooking liquid or canned chicken broth

¼ teaspoon salt

⅛ teaspoon freshly ground black pepper

BABY BEETS AND SWISS CHARD

2 tablespoons unsalted butter

16 baby gold beets, greens trimmed leaving ¼-inch stems, scrubbed

¼ teaspoon salt

⅛ teaspoon freshly ground black pepper

1 pound Swiss chard, rinsed and dried, tough stems removed

1 tablespoon sherry-wine vinegar

ROSE PETAL MOLE

½ cup Mole Poblano (see recipe, page 199), made with Lamb Stock (see recipe, page 188) instead of Chicken Stock

1 to 2 teaspoons honey

1 to 2 tablespoons rose water

LAMB

4 pieces lamb sirloin or boneless leg of lamb (about 7 ounces each), trimmed and cut into steaks

2 tablespoons canola oil

½ teaspoon salt

¼ teaspoon freshly ground black pepper

Chive Oil (optional; see recipe, page 190)

Cordero en Mole Verde

Lamb Shank in Green Mole with Roasted Vegetables

Makes 4 servings

Hulled pumpkin seeds help to thicken the tomatillo-based sauce. But the real secret to this dish is to braise the lamb long enough so the meat is falling off the bone.

Lamb Shanks In a large pot, heat the oil. Season the lamb shanks with the salt and pepper. Add the shanks to the hot oil and sear on all sides until browned, 10 to 12 minutes. Transfer the shanks to a plate.

Mole Verde Pour off all but 1 tablespoon fat from the pot. Add the tomatillos, onion, garlic, and chiles, and sauté, scraping up any browned bits from the bottom of the pot with a wooden spoon, until the tomatillos and onion are lightly browned and the onion is softened, about 5 minutes. Stir in the pumpkin seeds. Return the lamb shanks to the pot. Add the 2 cups water and the white wine. Bring to a boil. Lower the heat, cover the pot, and simmer until the meat is very tender, 2 to 3 hours. Check the liquid level from time to time to make sure the mixture doesn't get too dry.

Transfer the lamb shanks to a baking dish, cover, and keep warm in a low oven. Strain the cooking liquid through a medium sieve placed over a large bowl—discard the liquid or save for making soup. Spoon the solids into a blender and puree. Strain through a medium sieve placed over a clean bowl, and then press on the solids with a rubber spatula to release more liquid and push through the soft solids. Pour the liquid into a large skillet, add the stock, and gently boil, stirring occasionally, until the sauce is thickened, about 5 minutes. Season with honey, salt, and pepper. Keep the sauce warm in the skillet.

Vegetables In a clean, large skillet, heat the oil over medium heat. Add the carrots, potato, and chayote. Cover the skillet and cook until

the vegetables are crisp-tender, 10 to 15 minutes. Add the vegetables to the mole sauce.

To serve Into each of 4 large soup bowls, spoon some of the sauce and vegetables. Place a lamb shank in each bowl and spoon some sauce over the top. If desired, sprinkle with sesame seeds and decorate with drizzles of the Guajillo Chile Oil.

LAMB SHANKS

2 tablespoons canola oil

4 lamb shanks (about the top two-thirds of the shanks, 3 to 4 pounds total)

½ teaspoon salt

¼ teaspoon freshly ground black pepper

MOLE VERDE

20 tomatillos, papery husks removed, rinsed well, halved if large

1 onion, chopped

1 clove garlic, chopped

2 fresh serrano chiles, stems removed

½ cup hulled, unsalted pumpkin seeds

2 cups water

3 tablespoons dry white wine

⅔ cup Chicken Stock (see recipe, page 186) or canned chicken broth

1 to 2 teaspoons honey, depending on size and hotness of serrano chiles

¼ teaspoon salt

⅛ teaspoon freshly ground black pepper

VEGETABLES

1 tablespoon canola oil

8 baby carrots, trimmed and peeled

1 potato, peeled and diced

1 chayote, peeled, pitted, and diced

GARNISH (optional)

Black sesame seeds

Guajillo Chile Oil (see recipe, page 190)

Champiñones Envueltos

Mushroom Strudel with Sweet Potato Puree

Makes 4 servings

MUSHROOM FILLING

2 teaspoons canola oil

½ pound shiitake mushrooms, stemmed and cleaned, caps thinly sliced

½ pound portobello mushrooms, stemmed and cleaned, caps thinly sliced

½ pound white button mushrooms, stemmed and cleaned, caps thinly sliced

1 small clove garlic, finely chopped

1 to 2 tablespoons Adobo (see recipe, page 192)

1 tablespoon chopped fresh chives

½ teaspoon chopped fresh thyme

½ teaspoon salt

Pinch freshly ground white pepper

STRUDEL

12 sheets phyllo dough, thawed if frozen

¼ cup (½ stick) unsalted butter, melted

1½ teaspoons chopped fresh chives

¼ teaspoon salt

¼ teaspoon freshly ground black pepper

SWEET POTATO PUREE

1 sweet potato, peeled and cut into cubes

¼ teaspoon salt

Pinch freshly ground white pepper

ARUGULA SALAD

½ pound arugula, cleaned and stemmed

2 teaspoons freshly squeezed lemon juice

¼ teaspoon salt

⅛ teaspoon freshly ground black pepper

GARNISH (optional)

Habanero–Red Bell Pepper Reduction (see recipe, page 189)

Pomegranate Juice Reduction (see recipe, page 189)

Chive Oil (see recipe, page 190)

You can serve this as an appetizer or an entrée and, with the right filling, even as a dessert. That points to what I especially like about this dish: the phyllo can be stuffed with anything, from grilled vegetables to shredded beef to pears accompanied by a chocolate sauce.

Mushroom Filling In a large skillet, heat the oil over medium heat. Working in batches if necessary, add the mushrooms and garlic to the skillet and cook, stirring occasionally, until the mushrooms release their liquid and are lightly colored, 5 to 10 minutes per batch—you should have a total of about 3 cups cooked mushrooms. Stir in the Adobo to taste, the chives, thyme, salt, and pepper. Cook, stirring, for 1 minute. Remove the skillet from the heat and set aside.

Strudel Preheat the oven to 350°F. On a flat, clean work surface, unfold the phyllo. Lift off 1 sheet from the stack and lay it flat. Brush lightly with melted butter. Season with a little of the chives, salt, and pepper. Repeat the layering with 5 more phyllo sheets, buttering and seasoning each sheet as before, for a total of 6 layers. (Keep the main stack of phyllo covered with damp paper towels to prevent them from drying out while you're making the strudel.) Spoon half the mushroom filling lengthwise down the center of the phyllo. Snugly roll up the phyllo around the filling. Dampen the long edge of the seam with water and press against the roll to seal. Place the roll, seam side down, on an ungreased baking sheet. Repeat with the remaining phyllo and filling and place on the baking sheet.

Bake for 45 minutes, or until the phyllo is lightly colored and flaky, and the mushroom filling is heated through. Transfer the rolls to a wire rack and let rest.

Sweet Potato Puree While the strudel is baking, in a saucepan of boiling water, cook the sweet potato until tender, about 30 minutes. Drain, reserving the cooking liquid. Transfer

the sweet potato cubes to a small food processor. Season with salt and white pepper. Add a little of the cooking liquid and process until pureed. With the motor running, gradually add more cooking liquid until a smooth, firm puree is formed. Transfer to a small saucepan and keep warm.

Arugula Salad In a large bowl, toss together the arugula, lemon juice, salt, and pepper.

To serve In the center of each of 4 dinner plates, spread a quarter of the sweet potato puree. Arrange the arugula salad over the top. Cut each of the strudel rolls into fourths, so each piece has one end that has been cut diagonally. In the center of each plate, stand 2 phyllo pieces upright, pointed ends up. If desired, decorate the plates with the Habanero–Red Bell Pepper Reduction, Pomegranate Juice Reduction, and Chive Oil.

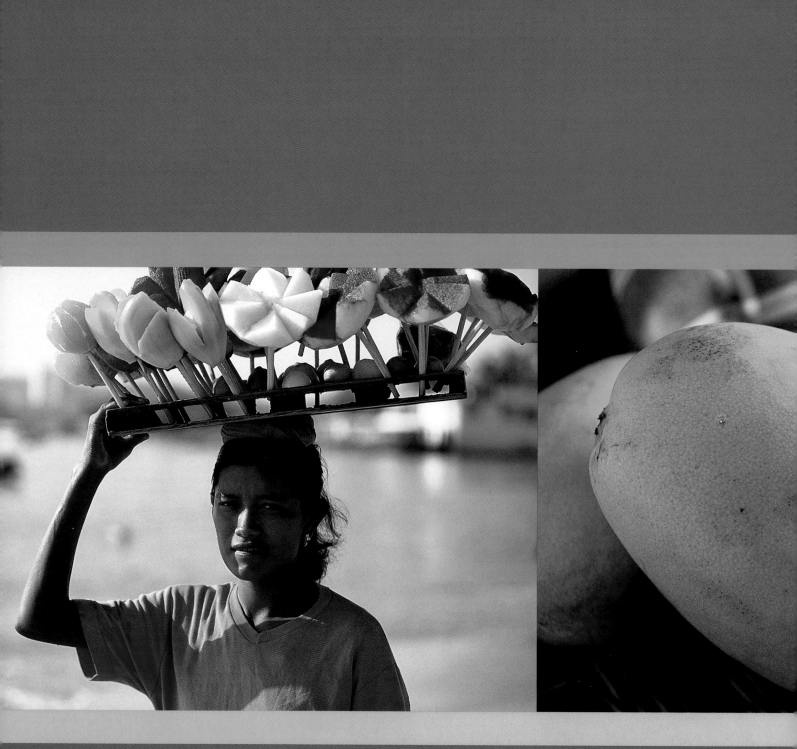

Desserts

Tamal de Chocolate

Chocolate Tamale with Hazelnut Sauce

Makes 8 servings

HAZELNUT SAUCE
1 cup milk

2 teaspoons sugar

2 large egg yolks

½ teaspoon hazelnut paste

PHYLLO "CORN HUSKS"
4 sheets phyllo dough, thawed if frozen

¼ cup (½ stick) unsalted butter, melted

CHOCOLATE TAMALES
1 cup chopped good-quality bittersweet
     chocolate

1 cup (2 sticks) unsalted butter, cut into small
     pieces

½ cup sugar

1 large egg, lightly beaten

1 cup all-purpose flour

8 large dried corn husks

GARNISH (optional)
Cinnamon ice cream

Crema fresca mixed with a little sugar, or
     crème fraîche, stirred

Chocolate Sauce (see recipe, page 207)

Fresh blackberries

(Pages 168 to 169) A woman offers cooling mango,
papaya, jícama, and watermelon (left) along the
beach in Acapulco. The mango Manila (center) is
only one of the hundreds of different mango varieties.
Baskets of fresh breads (right) are sold in the
markets in Valle de Bravo, a relaxing get-away to the
west of Mexico City that attracts hundreds of
thousands of migrating monarch butterflies each year.

There are many different kinds of tamales, including ones for dessert. As with all tamales, you can serve this warm right out of the steamer. Or it can be made ahead, refrigerated for up to three days, and then resteamed just before serving, or rewarmed in a microwave oven.

Hazelnut Sauce In a small saucepan, boil together the milk and sugar, stirring until sugar is dissolved. In a small bowl, lightly beat the yolks. Stir in a little of the hot milk mixture. Stir the egg yolk mixture into the milk mixture in the saucepan. Over very low heat, cook, stirring, until thick enough to coat the back of a spoon, 1 to 2 minutes—be careful not to let mixture boil or the sauce will curdle. Pour into a bowl. In a cup, stir together hazelnut paste and a little of the hot milk mixture. Stir into the bowl. Let cool, then refrigerate to chill.

Phyllo "Corn Husks" Preheat the oven to 250°F. Place a phyllo sheet on a flat surface. Brush with butter. Layer on the remaining 3 sheets of phyllo, brushing each layer with butter. Cut the stack of sheets into quarters (in half across the width and length). Then cut each quarter in half crosswise. Pinch one end and wrap a small strip of aluminum foil around the pinch, spreading the other end to resemble a corn husk. Place on a baking sheet. Repeat with the remaining pieces for a total of 8 phyllo "corn husks." Bake until light golden, about 15 minutes. Transfer the phyllo to a wire rack to cool.

Chocolate Tamales In a medium saucepan, melt together the chocolate, butter, and sugar over medium-low heat. Remove from the heat. In a small bowl, lightly beat the egg. Stir a little of the hot chocolate mixture into the egg. Stir the egg mixture into the chocolate mixture in the saucepan. Stir in the flour until well blended. Scrape into a clean bowl and let stand until set.

In a bowl of warm water, soak the dried corn husks until softened, about 30 minutes. Drain and pat the husks dry with paper towels.

To fill (see photos, page 69) Spread a corn husk out on a flat work surface. Spread about ½ cup of the chocolate mixture over the lower, wide end of the husk, leaving a ¾-inch border on either side and 1½ inches at the pointed end. Bring the two long sides of the husk up and over the chocolate, overlapping the long sides of the husk. Fold the pointed end up. Repeat with the remaining 7 husks. Place the tamales, folded end down, in a steamer insert. (The insert needs to be about 4 inches deep. If it is wide, steady the tamales against the sides by placing a ball of aluminum foil in the center.) Add 1 to 2 inches of water to the pot. Place the insert in the pot, cover, and steam over low heat for about 40 minutes. (Check the water level from time to time.) When done, the husks can be easily peeled away from the filling. Remove the steamer from the heat and let the tamales remain in the steamer 2 to 3 minutes to allow the filling to become firm.

To serve Remove the corn husk from the tamales. Remove the aluminum foil from the phyllo. In the center of each of 8 dinner plates, spoon a pool of hazelnut sauce. Place a phyllo "husk" in the pool. Place a chocolate tamal on top of the phyllo. If desired, garnish the plate with the ice cream, crema fresca, Chocolate Sauce, and blackberries.

Empanadas de Plátano

Banana-Filled Turnovers

Makes 8 servings

2 bananas, peeled and chopped

¼ cup walnuts, chopped

1 teaspoon crema fresca or crème fraîche, stirred (or sour cream mixed with a little heavy cream)

½ teaspoon sugar

1 package (17.25 ounces) puff pastry, thawed following package directions

2 large eggs, lightly beaten

Canola oil, for frying

GARNISH (optional)

Crema fresca mixed with a little sugar, or crème fraîche, stirred

Shredded unsweetened coconut, toasted

Raspberry Sauce (see recipe, page 207)

Coconut ice cream

4 fresh strawberries, halved

A very popular and simple dessert in Mexico consists of nothing more than sliced bananas with a little cream and sugar. That was my starting point. I just added some chopped walnuts and puff pastry, and transformed the whole thing into little empanadas.

In a medium bowl, stir together the banana, walnuts, crema fresca, and sugar. Set aside.

Unfold one of the puff pastry sheets. Using a 4-inch round cookie cutter or pastry cutter, cut out 4 circles from the sheet. Brush each circle with a little of the eggs. Slightly off center on each circle, spoon about 1 tablespoon of the banana mixture. Fold one side over the filling and crimp the edges together to seal. Place on a sheet of waxed paper. Repeat with the remaining sheet of puff pastry and filling.

In a large, deep saucepan, heat 3 to 4 inches of oil until it registers about 350°F. on a deep-fat frying thermometer. Working in batches, fry the empanadas, turning over from time to time with a slotted spoon, until crisp and golden brown, 5 to 10 minutes. With a slotted spoon, transfer the empanadas to a rack set over paper towels to drain.

To serve Cut the warm empanadas in half, and on each of 8 dinner plates, arrange an empanada. If desired, garnish the plates with crema fresca, toasted coconut, Raspberry Sauce, ice cream, and strawberries.

Flan de Caramelo

Flan with Caramel Sauce

Makes 8 individual flans

Practically every restaurant and every household in Mexico has its own version of flan. The recipe here is the result of constant tinkering. I began with a flan taught to me by Señor Huerta, a chef who helped me open my first restaurant many years ago—an Italian restaurant in Mexico. Señor Huerta was in his fifties and I was in my twenties, so you can imagine how much I learned from this man. When I first opened Maya restaurant in New York City, one of my pastry chefs there taught me his version, so the experimenting continued.

CARAMEL
½ cup sugar
¼ cup water

CUSTARD
2 cups milk
1 cup sugar
½ vanilla pod
4 large eggs

GARNISH (optional)
Caramel Sauce (see recipe, page 208)

Preheat the oven to 350°F.

Caramel In a small skillet, stir together the sugar and the water. Bring to a boil, stirring to dissolve the sugar. Continue to gently boil, without stirring, until amber colored, about 5 minutes. Spoon a little of the caramel into eight ½-cup ramekins or aluminum foil cupcake pans. Carefully swirl each ramekin as you pour, to evenly coat the bottom. Reserve the remaining caramel to garnish the finished dishes.

Custard In a medium saucepan, combine the milk, sugar, and vanilla pod. Bring to a boil, stirring to dissolve the sugar. Remove from the heat and remove the vanilla pod. In a small bowl, whisk the eggs until well blended. Whisk a little of the hot milk mixture into the eggs. Then whisk the egg mixture into the milk mixture in the saucepan. Pour the mixture into the prepared ramekins, dividing equally.

Place the ramekins in a baking dish on the middle rack in the oven. Pour enough hot water into the pan to come halfway up the sides of the ramekins. Bake for 40 to 50 minutes, until a small knife inserted into a center of a flan comes out clean. Remove the ramekins from the water bath and transfer to a wire rack to cool. Then refrigerate, covered, for 4 hours or overnight. The flans can be refrigerated for up to 3 days.

Garnish If desired, on a large piece of waxed paper, drizzle the Caramel Sauce in 8 circular patterns, about 2 inches in diameter. Let harden. Carefully peel off the waxed paper.

To serve In the center of a large dinner plate, unmold a flan, letting the caramel in the bottom of the ramekin run down the sides of the flan. If desired, gently reheat the remaining caramel and spoon a little around the flan. If using the caramel garnish, insert it in the top of the flan. Repeat with the remaining flans.

Flan de Tamarindo

Tamarind Flan

Makes 8 individual flans

CARAMEL
½ cup sugar
¼ cup water

CUSTARD
2 cups milk
1 cup sugar
2 tablespoons tamarind paste
4 large eggs

Vanilla Sauce (see recipe, page 208)

GARNISH (optional)
12 maraschino cherries, halved
Fresh mint leaves
Crisp Tortilla Strips (see recipe, page 204)

After a heavy meal, this is the perfect finish. Even though the flan is rich, the tart tamarind flavor has a cleansing effect on the taste buds.

reheat the oven to 350°F.

Caramel In a small skillet, combine the sugar and the water. Bring to a boil, stirring to dissolve the sugar, and continue to gently boil, without stirring, until amber colored, about 5 minutes. Spoon a little of the caramel into the bottoms of eight ½-cup ramekins or aluminum foil cupcake cups. Reserve the remaining caramel to garnish the finished dishes.

Custard In a medium saucepan, combine the milk and sugar. Bring to a gentle boil, stirring to dissolve the sugar. In a small bowl, with the back of a spoon, mash together the tamarind paste with a little of the hot milk. Stir into the milk mixture in the saucepan. Remove from the heat and whisk vigorously to incorporate the tamarind. Strain the mixture through a medium-mesh sieve into a bowl. Discard the solids in the sieve.

In a small bowl, lightly beat the eggs. Stir in a little of the hot milk mixture. Stir the egg mixture into the milk in the saucepan and whisk to combine. Pour the mixture into the prepared ramekins, dividing equally. Place the cups in a baking pan on the middle rack in the oven. Pour enough hot water into the baking pan to come halfway up the sides of the ramekins. Bake until the flans are just set, 30 to 40 minutes. Remove the ramekins from the water bath and transfer to a wire rack. Let cool. Refrigerate until thoroughly chilled, about 4 hours or overnight.

To serve Gently heat the remaining caramel. In the center of each of 8 dinner plates, carefully unmold a flan, letting the caramel drip down the sides. Spoon a little Vanilla Sauce around the flan along with the remaining caramel. If desired, garnish the plates with maraschino cherry halves and the flans with mint leaves, and stick the Crisp Tortilla Strips upright in the flans.

Tamal de Cajeta

Caramel Tamale with Vanilla Sauce

Makes 6 tamales

The caramel of the cajeta lightly accented by the faint flavor of the corn husk makes this dessert tamale unique. The filling mixture is a little soft, so make sure to tightly wrap the husk before steaming to avoid any leakage. Like the Tamal de Chocolate, (see recipe, page 170), the tamales can be steamed ahead, refrigerated and then resteamed or heated in a microwave oven just before serving.

TAMALE FILLING

1½ cups all-purpose flour
½ cup granulated sugar
¼ cup (½ stick) unsalted butter, melted
1 large egg, lightly beaten
1 cup milk
1 cup bottled cajeta (goat's milk caramel)

6 large dried corn husks

1 cup Vanilla Sauce (see recipe, page 208)
1 cup bottled cajeta (goat's milk caramel), warmed

GARNISH (optional)
¼ cup finely diced fresh peach
Fresh strawberries
Shredded fresh mint

Tamale Filling In a medium bowl, with an electric mixer fitted with the whisk attachment, on low speed, combine the flour and sugar. On medium speed, beat in the melted butter and egg until well blended and the mixture is crumbly. Gradually beat in the milk until thoroughly blended, and then the cajeta—the caramel mixture will form ribbons on itself when the beater is turned off and lifted. Cover and refrigerate overnight.

Soak the corn husks in a bowl of warm water to soften, about 30 minutes.

To fill (see photos, page 69) Drain the corn husks and pat dry with the paper towels. Spread a corn husk out on a flat work surface. Spread about ½ cup of the filling over the lower, wide end of the husk, leaving a ¾-inch border on either side and 1½ inches at the pointed end. Bring the two long sides of the husk up and over the filling, overlapping the long sides of the husk. Fold the pointed end up. Make sure all the seams are tight to avoid any leakage during steaming. Place the tamale, folded end down, in a steamer insert. (The insert needs to be about 4 inches deep. If the insert is wide, steady the tamales against the sides by placing a ball of aluminum foil in the center of the insert.) Repeat with the remaining husks and filling. Add 1 to 2 inches of water to the pot. Place the insert in the pot, cover, and steam over low heat for about 30 to 40 minutes. (Check the water level from time to time.) When the tamales are done, the husks can be easily peeled away from the filling. Remove the steamer from the heat and let the tamales remain in the steamer for 2 to 3 minutes to allow the filling to become firm.

To serve Remove the corn husks from the tamales. In the center of each of 6 dinner plates, spoon a little Vanilla Sauce. Place a tamale in each pool and drizzle some warmed cajeta over each tamale. If desired, garnish with the peach, strawberries, and mint.

Crepas de Cajeta

Warm Crepes with Caramel Sauce

Makes 4 servings

This crepe dessert (pictured, opposite page) is surprisingly simple to prepare, and all the elements—the crepes, the caramel sauce, and the candied walnuts—can be made ahead. Once you have even a small taste of the sauce, you'll understand why people can't get enough.

1 cup milk
¾ cup bottled cajeta (goat's milk caramel)
12 Crepes (see recipe, page 208)
12 Candied Walnuts (see recipe, page 208)

GARNISH (optional)
4 Tuiles (see recipe, page 209)
Cinnamon ice cream

In a medium saucepan, combine the milk and cajeta. Bring to a boil, stirring occasionally to dissolve the caramel. Lower the heat to keep the sauce warm. (The sauce can be made ahead, cooled, and stored, tightly covered, in the refrigerator for up to 1 week. To serve, reheat.)

Fold each crepe in half, and then in half again. Add to the sauce to heat through.

To serve On each of 4 dinner plates, arrange 3 of the crepes spoke-fashion. Spoon some extra sauce over the crepes. Place a Candied Walnut on each crepe. If desired, place a Tuile in the center of each plate and fill with a small scoop of ice cream.

Crepas de Chocolate

Crepes with Chocolate Sauce

Makes 4 servings

A variation of the Crepas de Cajeta (see recipe, above), these crepes with chocolate sauce actually have a connection to my childhood. One of my favorite treats used to be pancakes with chocolate atole, a hot drink made from corn flour—a combination of flavors not unlike those of this dessert.

Chocolate Sauce (see recipe, page 207)
12 Crepes (see recipe, page 208)

GARNISH (optional)
4 Tuiles (see recipe, page 209)
Cinnamon ice cream

In a large skillet, gently heat the Chocolate Sauce. Fold each crepe in half, and then in half again. Add the crepes to the sauce and gently heat the crepes.

To serve On each of 4 dinner plates, arrange 3 crepes spoke-fashion. Spoon any remaining sauce over the crepes. If desired, garnish with a Tuile filled with a small scoop of ice cream.

Pastel de Coco y Queso

Coconut Cheesecake

Makes 4 individual cheesecakes

Coconuts are abundant in Acapulco, and they are processed into a whole range of products, including everything from tanning oils to sweets. My favorite was the coconut paste sold on the streets. The cheesecake here is inspired by the memory of that taste.

COCONUT CHEESECAKES

1 package (8 ounces) cream cheese, at room temperature

½ cup sugar

1 large egg

⅓ cup finely grated unsweetened coconut

GARNISH (optional)

2 Tuiles (see recipe, page 209)

½ cup Raspberry Sauce (see recipe, page 207)

Shredded unsweetened coconut, toasted

Preheat the oven to 325°F. Butter four ½-cup ramekins or foil cupcake pans.

Coconut Cheesecakes Using an electric mixer with a paddle attachment, in a medium bowl beat the cream cheese until creamy. Beat in the sugar until well blended, and then the egg. Beat in the coconut. Spoon the batter into the buttered cups, dividing equally. Place the cups in a baking pan on the center rack in the oven. Pour enough hot water into the roasting pan to come halfway up the sides of the cups.

Bake until set, about 35 minutes. Remove the cups from the water bath and transfer to a wire rack and let cool. Refrigerate until chilled, about 4 hours or overnight. The cheesecakes can be refrigerated for up to 3 days.

To serve In the center of each of 4 dinner plates, unmold a cheesecake. If garnishing, break the Tuiles into long wedges and insert in the top of the cheesecakes. Garnish with the Raspberry Sauce and coconut.

Mousse de Café de Olla

Frozen Coffee Mousse

Makes 10 servings

A popular Mexcian coffee, café de olla is made with orange zest, cinammon sticks, and piloncillo or dark brown sugar (see recipe, below). I wanted to turn the light, aromatic drink into a dessert—so here it is, as a frozen mousse.

8 large egg yolks
1 cup sugar
½ cup brewed espresso
2 cups heavy cream

GARNISH (optional)
Strawberries, sliced into fans
Caramel Sauce (see recipe, page 208)
Guava Sauce (see recipe, page 207)

Line the bottom of an 8- or 9-inch springform pan with a round of parchment paper or waxed paper.

In the top of a double boiler over simmering water, with a handheld electric mixer on medium speed, beat the egg yolks until thickened, 2 to 3 minutes. Gradually beat in the sugar until well blended. Gradually beat in the espresso. Continue to heat the mixture, gently stirring with a whisk, scraping the sides of the double boiler to keep the eggs from cooking on the sides, until the mixture registers 140°F. on an instant-read thermometer. Continue to gently whisk, scraping the sides, for another 3 minutes, adjusting the heat so the mixture remains at 140°F. Scrape the mixture into a clean bowl and let cool.

In a clean medium bowl, with clean beaters, beat the cream until soft peaks form. Fold into the cooled egg yolk mixture. Spoon into the springform pan. Place in the freezer until frozen solid, about 8 hours. The mousse can be stored, covered, in the freezer for up to 4 days.

To serve Run a thin knife around the inside of the pan. Release the side and remove. Slice the mousse into 20 equal wedges. Let stand until slightly softened, about 5 minutes. Arrange 2 wedges on a dinner plate for each serving. If desired, garnish with a strawberry, the Caramel Sauce, and Guava Sauce.

Café de Olla

Mexican Coffee

Makes 4 servings

This sweet, citrusy coffee (opposite page) goes well with many desserts. You can make the flavoring base ahead and store it, tightly covered, in the refrigerator for a couple of days. To serve, gently reheat it and add it to the freshly brewed coffee.

2 cups water
½ cup packed piloncillo (dark brown sugar)
Grated rind of ½ orange
2 cinnamon sticks, broken into pieces
3 cups hot, freshly brewed coffee

In a medium saucepan, combine the water, the pilconcillo, orange rind, and cinnamon sticks, and stir to dissolve the sugar. Bring to a boil and continue to gently boil until the liquid is reduced by half, 15 to 20 minutes. Strain the liquid, and combine with the coffee, and serve.

Basics

Black Beans

Makes about 4 cups cooked beans

Black beans, a personal favorite of mine, are part of practically every meal in Mexico, whether breakfast, dinner, or something else. Beans are a complement to almost every dish, which is why in my restaurants I serve them on the side with all entrées.

My method for cooking beans yields a large amount of cooking liquid or stock, which can then be saved and used for flavoring rice or as a base for sauces. The stock is also the beginning of the Black Bean Stock Reduction (see recipe, right), which makes a delicious sauce for fish.

Many think you can't make a pot of black beans without epazote, a green herb that grows wild in Mexico and the United States. Its slightly peppery, lemony taste is a delicious accent to the beans. During the summer and fall, you can find the herb in farmers' markets in this country.

½ cup chopped bacon
1 tablespoon lard or solid vegetable shortening
1 cup chopped white Spanish onion
1 cup epazote leaves or ¼ cup dried epazote (optional)
16 cups (1 gallon) Chicken Stock (see recipe, right) or water
½ pound dried black beans
½ teaspoon salt
¼ teaspoon freshly ground black pepper

In a large pot, heat the bacon and lard until the lard is melted and the bacon begins to render a little fat. Add the chopped onion and epazote leaves, if using, and sauté until the onion is softened, 10 to 15 minutes. Carefully add the stock. Cover and bring to a boil. Add the beans. Lower the heat and simmer, covered, until the beans are very tender, about 2 hours. The beans should be soupy—you should have about 13 cups liquid. Season with salt and pepper.

(Pages 184 to 185) The amazing variety of Mexico's produce includes plantains, mushrooms, and blackberries.

Black Bean Stock When a recipe calls for this, use the cooking liquid from the black beans. Store the cooking liquid, tightly covered, in the refrigerator for up to 3 days, or freeze for up to 2 months.

Black Bean Puree In a blender or food processor, puree the black beans, adding the black bean cooking liquid, water, or chicken broth as needed for desired consistency. A good proportion is ⅓ cup liquid to 1 cup cooked beans. Store, tightly covered, in the refrigerator for up to 3 days.

Black Bean Stock Reduction

Makes about 2 cups

This reduction on its own makes a wonderful sauce for pan-seared fish such as red snapper or halibut.

1 quart Black Bean Stock (see recipe, above)
1 quart Chicken Stock (see recipe, below)
1 tablespoon sherry-wine vinegar
1 tablespoon honey
½ teaspoon salt
¼ teaspoon freshly ground black pepper

In a large saucepan, combine the Black Bean Stock, Chicken Stock, vinegar, and honey. Gently boil over medium heat until reduced to 2 cups, about 1 hour and 15 minutes. Season with the salt and pepper. Store, tightly covered, in the refrigerator for up to 3 days, or freeze for up to 1 month.

Chicken Stock

Makes about 3 quarts (12 to 14 cups)

1 whole chicken, gizzard and innards removed
1 white Spanish onion, chopped
2 carrots, chopped
4 ribs celery, chopped
6 whole black peppercorns
1 bay leaf

In a stockpot, combine all the ingredients. Add just enough cold water to cover the chicken. Bring to a boil over high heat, then lower the heat and simmer, partially covered, for 3 hours, skimming the foam. Check the liquid level from time to time, making sure the chicken remains just covered. Transfer the chicken to a platter. Remove any chicken pieces that may remain in the pot. Working in batches if necessary, strain the stock through a large sieve set over a large bowl. Discard the solids in the sieve and let the stock cool. When the chicken is cool enough to handle, remove the skin and pull the meat from the bones. Discard the skin and bones, and refrigerate the meat, covered, for other uses. Refrigerate the stock, covered, overnight. Remove the solidified fat from the top and discard. Refrigerate the stock, covered, for up to 3 days, or freeze for up to 2 months.

Duck Stock

Makes about 2 quarts (about 8 cups)

When you have a leisurely afternoon on a weekend, plan to make a batch of this rich, flavorful stock. Roasting the bones and vegetables adds an extra depth of flavor to the finished product. I use the stock for my Pozole de Pato (see recipe, page 151), but it also works well in most hearty meat soups and stews.

1 tablespoon canola oil
1 carrot, peeled and chopped
1 small white Spanish onion, coarsely chopped
2 ribs celery, coarsely chopped
1 duck carcass (see Note)
2 whole black peppercorns
1 bay leaf

Preheat the oven to 400°F. In a small roasting pan, mix together the oil, carrot, onion, and celery. Place the carcass in the pan. Roast for 1 hour, stirring the vegetables occasionally.

Transfer the carcass with the vegetables to a stockpot. Add enough water to cover. Add the peppercorns and bay leaf. Bring to a boil over high heat. Lower the heat and simmer, partially covered, for 3 hours, skimming the foam. Check the liquid level from time to time, making sure the duck remains just covered. With a slotted spoon, remove the carcass and vegetables from the stock and discard. Working in batches if necessary, strain the stock through a large sieve set over a large bowl. Discard any solids in the sieve and let the stock cool. Refrigerate the stock, covered, overnight. Remove the solidified fat from the top and discard. Refrigerate the stock, covered, for up to 3 days, or freeze for up to 2 months.

Note Buy a whole duck—a fresh one if you can find it. Divide the duck into parts: 2 breasts, 2 legs and thighs, and 2 wings. The remaining carcass is used for the stock. The breasts can be used for Pozole de Pato (page 151) and the legs and thighs for Carnitas de Pato (page 101).

Duck Fat

Makes 4 cups

Sautéing vegetables or even cooking eggs in a little duck fat adds a delicious note. I use the fat to make confit for my Carnitas de Pato (see recipe, page 101). Good-quality duck fat can be purchased in specialty food stores and used as a substitute for the homemade.

Fat and skin of 2 ducks, cut into small pieces
½ cup water

In a heavy pot, combine the duck fat and skin and the water. Cover and simmer over low heat for 30 minutes. Uncover the pot and continue to cook over low heat until all the fat is melted into liquid, another hour. If you want cracklings or crisp skin, increase the heat to medium and continue to cook until the pieces of skin are golden brown and crisp—the fat will crackle. Scrape the bottom of the pan with a metal spatula from time to time to prevent the skin from sticking. Carefully strain the liquid through a medium-mesh sieve lined with a double thickness of paper towel placed over a large bowl. Let the fat cool, and the cracklings if you've made them. Store the fat, covered, and the cracklings, covered, in the refrigerator for up to 1 week, or freeze for up to 3 months.

Veal Stock

Makes about 3 quarts (12 cups)

3 pounds veal bones
1 white Spanish onion, chopped
1 carrot, chopped
4 ribs celery, chopped
6 black peppercorns
1 bay leaf
½ cup tomato paste

Preheat the oven to 400°F. Place the bones in a large roasting pan and roast until browned, stirring occasionally, about 1 hour. Put the bones in a stockpot and add the onion, carrot, celery, peppercorns, and bay leaf. In a small bowl, stir together the tomato paste and 1 cup water. Add to the stockpot along with enough water to cover the ingredients, about 14 cups total. Bring to a boil. Reduce the heat and simmer, uncovered, over very low heat for 2 hours. Check the liquid level from time to time, making sure the bones remain just covered. Skim the foam from the top occasionally, and discard.

With tongs, remove the bones from the stock and discard. Working in batches if necessary, strain the stock through a large sieve set over a large bowl. Discard the solids in the sieve and let the stock cool. Refrigerate the stock, covered, overnight. Remove the solidified fat from the top and discard. Refrigerate the stock, covered, for up to 3 days, or freeze for up to 2 months.

Lamb Stock Substitute 3 pounds lamb bones for the veal bones.

Boiled Lobster

Makes 2 cups cooked lobster meat

2 live lobsters (1¼ to 1½ pounds each)

Bring a large pot of water to a boil. Slide the lobsters, claws first, into the boiling water. Boil for about 10 minutes if you plan to cook the lobster meat in another recipe. Otherwise, cook for about 12 minutes, or until the shells are bright orange-red, the tails are curled, and the antennae can be removed easily. Remove the lobsters from the water and let cool. Remove the meat and save the shells and carcasses for broth (see Lobster Broth, below).

Lobster Broth

Makes about 2 quarts (about 8 cups)

Use this flavorful broth as the starting point for seafood soups and sauces.

1 tablespoon canola oil
2 lobster carcasses with shells (see Boiled Lobster, above)
1 white Spanish onion, chopped
1 carrot, chopped
1 rib celery, chopped
1 tablespoon tomato paste
2 quarts water
6 whole black peppercorns
1 bay leaf

In a large saucepan, heat the oil. Add the lobster carcasses and shells, onion, carrot, and celery. Sauté until the vegetables are lightly browned, about 4 minutes. Meanwhile, in a measuring cup, dissolve the tomato paste in about ¼ cup of the water. Add the dissolved tomato paste, peppercorns, and bay leaf to the saucepan. Stir in the remaining water. Simmer, partially covered, for 1 hour. Strain and let cool. Store the broth, tightly covered, in the refrigerator, for up to 3 days, or freeze for up to 1 month.

Bell Pepper Juice

Makes about 2 cups

I use this pepper extract to flavor sauces, and the color of the liquid itself makes it a colorful garnish to drizzle over plates.

2 pounds (about 4 large) bell peppers, red or yellow

Stem and seed the peppers. Remove the membranes. Place the peppers in a blender and puree. Strain through a fine-mesh sieve set over a bowl, pressing on the solids with a rubber spatula. Discard the solids. Store the juice, tightly covered, in the refrigerator for up to 5 days.

Balsamic Vinegar–Adobo Sauce

Makes ½ cup

This bittersweet vinegar reduction is a flavorful garnish and can be drizzled over just about anything, including seafood and even salads. In my Chuleta de Puerco en Vinagre Balsamico (see recipe, page 152), I serve a stuffed pork chop in a pool of the reduction.

3 cups balsamic vinegar
2 tablespoons Adobo (see recipe, page 192)
1 tablespoon heavy cream
¼ teaspoon salt

In a medium saucepan, combine the vinegar, Adobo, and heavy cream (the cream may look curdled). Gently boil until reduced to ½ cup, about 20 minutes. Add the salt. Store, tightly covered, in the refrigerator for up to 3 days.

Habanero–Red Bell Pepper Reduction

Makes about ⅔ cup

The sweetness of this sauce with its touch of heat nicely complements crabmeat and shrimp without overpowering the richness of the seafood.

4 pounds red bell peppers, stemmed, seeded, membranes removed, and cut into chunks

1 fresh habanero chile

¼ teaspoon salt

⅛ teaspoon freshly ground black pepper

Working in batches, puree the red bell peppers in a blender. Strain through a sieve placed over a bowl, pressing on the solids with a rubber spatula (you should have about 4 cups juice). Discard the solids. Combine the juice with the chile in a medium saucepan. Gently boil over medium heat until reduced to about ⅔ cup, about 30 minutes. Remove the chile and discard. Season the reduction with the salt and pepper. Store, tightly covered, in the refrigerator for up to 3 days.

Pomegranate Juice Reduction

Makes about ½ cup

Used as a garnish, this reduction, with its sweet, acidic kick and astringent overtones, goes well with dishes that need a little boost, and it stands up to spicy foods as well. When pomegranates (pictured at right) are in season, we use fresh juice, but to make things easier in the home kitchen, pomegranate juice is now available in bottles. The reduction keeps well in the refrigerator for a week or two.

1 quart pomegranate juice

In a medium saucepan, gently boil the pomegranate juice until reduced to about ½ cup, about 40 minutes. Let cool. Store, tightly covered, in the refrigerator for up to 2 weeks. Serve at room temperature or gently reheated.

Blood Orange Reduction

Makes about ⅔ cup

The concentrated tart-sweetness of this reduction makes a surprising accent to salads and pork, chicken, and strongly flavored fish dishes.

1 quart blood orange juice or regular orange juice

In a saucepan, boil the orange juice until reduced to about ⅔ cup—the liquid should be thick enough to hold its shape when spooned on a cooled plate. Let the juice cool. Store, tightly covered, in the refrigerator for up to 3 days.

Blood Orange–Chipotle Reduction Add 1 chipotle chile in adobo to the orange juice and reduce as directed above. Discard the chile.

Oils and Emulsions

Chive Oil

Makes about 1 cup

A little drizzle of this green oil dresses up any plate, and the chive flavor marries well with practically any food, ranging from seafood to chicken to salads. And it also works great in vinaigrettes. The Epazote Oil variation has a slightly sharper taste, but it can be used in the same way, as well as the Cilantro Oil.

1 cup canola oil
¼ cup snipped fresh chives

In a blender, process together the oil and chives. Store, tightly covered, in the refrigerator for up to 1 week. Let come to room temperature before using.

Epazote Oil For the chives, substitute a half bunch of fresh epazote, rinsed, dried, and coarsely chopped.

Cilantro Oil For the chives, substitute ¼ cup chopped fresh cilantro.

Lemon Oil

Makes about 1¼ cups

I like to drizzle a little of this over gazpacho, such as Gazpacho con Langosta (see recipe, page 57), as well as over salads and fish dishes.

1 cup olive oil
¼ cup freshly squeezed lemon juice (about 2 lemons)
¼ teaspoon salt
⅛ teaspoon freshly ground black pepper

In a small bowl or jar with a tight-fitting lid, mix all the ingredients together. Store, covered, in the refrigerator for up to 1 week. Let come to room temperature before using.

Guajillo Chile Oil

Makes ½ cup

The heat from this oil slowly sneaks up on you, so use it sparingly as a garnish. For extra zing, drizzle it over fish dishes, such as Ceviche de Atún (see recipe, page 32) and Tiritas de Pescado (see recipe, page 75; pictured at left). It also works well in strongly flavored combinations, such as Cordero en Mole Verde (see recipe, page 165).

½ cup canola oil
2 dried guajillo chiles, stems, seeds, and membranes removed, chiles broken into pieces

In a blender, combine the oil and the chiles. Blend until the chiles are finely ground. Store in a glass container, tightly covered, in the refrigerator for up 1 week. Let come to room temperature before using.

Pasilla Chile Oil

Makes ½ cup

Like the Guajillo Chile Oil, the heat of this oil also makes an impression. I drizzle a little of this on the plate with Terrina de Salmón Tartar (see recipe, page 94). Try it as a garnish with dishes featuring meats.

½ cup canola oil
2 dried pasilla chiles, stems, seeds, and membranes removed, chiles broken into pieces

In a blender, combine the oil and the chiles. Blend until the chiles are finely ground. Store in a glass container, tightly covered, in the refrigerator for up 1 week. Let come to room temperature before using.

Pasilla Chile Emulsion

Makes about 1 cup

To make an emulsion, oil is whisked or blended into the chile-flavored base until it is thoroughly incorporated and the mixture is thick and smooth.

4 cups Chicken Stock (see recipe, page 186) or
    ½ cup canned chicken broth
5 dried pasilla chile peppers, stems, seeds, and membranes
    removed, chiles broken into large pieces
½ cup canola oil
½ teaspoon sherry-wine vinegar
½ teaspoon honey, or more depending on the
    hotness of the chiles
½ teaspoon salt
¼ teaspoon freshly ground black pepper

If using homemade stock, pour the stock into a medium saucepan and boil until reduced to about ½ cup, about 20 minutes.

Heat a medium skillet over medium heat. Add the chile pieces and toast them until slightly colored, turning over once, 30 to 45 seconds. Transfer to a plate.

Pour the ½ cup stock or broth into a blender. Add the chile pieces and puree until very finely chopped. Strain through a fine sieve over a small bowl, pushing on the solids with the back of a ladle or a rubber spatula to release the liquid—you should have about ⅓ cup. Discard the solids. Pour the liquid into the blender.

With the blender running, slowly add the oil in a thin drizzle until an emulsion or slightly thick sauce forms—the oil should be thoroughly incorporated. Add the vinegar, honey, salt, and pepper, and blend. Store, tightly covered, in the refrigerator for up to 3 days. Shake or whisk well before using.

Guajillo Chile Emulsion

Makes about 1 cup

The color of this chile sauce reminds me of the sunny orange walls that you frequently see in Mexico. To make this emulsion, oil is whisked or blended into the adobo-flavored base until it is thoroughly incorporated and the mixture is thick and smooth. In my Halibut con Pepitas (see recipe, page 131), I spoon a little of the sauce over the caramelized chayote. It would also be delicious with crab cakes, or in fact, with any other fish or shellfish dish.

4 cups Chicken Stock (see recipe, page 186)
    or ⅓ cup canned chicken broth
½ cup canola oil
¼ cup Adobo (see recipe, page 192)
1 to 2 teaspoons sherry-wine vinegar
1 to 2 teaspoons honey
¼ teaspoon salt

If using homemade stock, pour the stock into a medium saucepan and boil until reduced to about ⅓ cup, about 20 minutes. Pour the ⅓ cup stock or broth into a blender. With the machine running, slowly add the oil in a thin drizzle until an emulsion forms. Add the adobo, vinegar, honey, and salt. Store, tightly covered, in the refrigerator for up to 3 days. Shake or whisk well before using.

Red Bell Pepper–Coriander Seed Emulsion

Makes about 1 cup

The technique for making an emulsion is the same as creating a thick vinaigrette or salad dressing. The emulsion is tasty as a garnish drizzled over plates, or as a dressing tossed with salad greens.

1½ cups Bell Pepper Juice (see recipe, page 188,
    using red bell peppers)
1 to 2 teaspoons sherry-wine vinegar
1 to 2 teaspoons honey
¼ teaspoon coriander seeds, crushed
¼ teaspoon salt
⅛ teaspoon freshly ground black pepper
½ cup canola oil

In a small saucepan, gently boil the Bell Pepper Juice until reduced by about half, about 15 minutes. Pour into a blender. Add the vinegar, honey, coriander, salt, and pepper. With the blender running, slowly add the oil in a thin drizzle until an emulsion forms. Adjust the seasonings as desired. Store the sauce, tightly covered, in the refrigerator for up to 3 days.

Achiote

Makes about ½ cup

Very often when you see a Mexican or Latin American sauce that is dark orange, annatto or achiote seeds from the annatto tree may be creating the color. This Achiote seasoning is used in the same way as my Adobo (see recipe, left), on its own or as the base of other sauces. It's particularly good for marinating meats, especially wild game. When mixed with citrus juices, it's very tasty with fish. As with the Adobo, you can make a large batch of this and store it in the refrigerator for several weeks. The sauce recipe following the achiote is one used in the Mixiote de Cordero (see recipe, page 160).

2 dried guajillo chiles
1 very small clove garlic, peeled
¼ cup water
2 tablespoons distilled white vinegar
2 tablespoons annatto seeds or annato paste
⅛ teaspoon cumin seeds
10 whole black peppercorns
3 whole cloves
¼ teaspoon salt

Remove the stems, seeds, and membranes from the chiles. Break the chiles into small pieces. In a blender, combine the chiles, garlic, the water, vinegar, annatto seeds, cumin seeds, peppercorns, cloves, and salt. Blend until pureed. Store, tightly covered, in the refrigerator for several weeks.

Achiote Sauce In a small skillet, heat 2 tablespoons butter. Stir in the Achiote (see recipe, above) and simmer for 2 minutes. Stir in ⅓ cup Veal Stock (see recipe, page 187), Chicken Stock (see recipe, page 186), canned chicken broth, or water, and simmer for 2 minutes. Stir in ¼ cup orange juice and simmer for 1 minute. Stir in 1 tablespoon honey, or more depending on the spiciness of the sauce, and ½ teaspoon salt, and simmer for 1 minute. If not using right away, allow the sauce to cool, and then store, tightly covered, in the refrigerator for a couple of weeks. Makes about 1 cup.

Adobo

Makes about ½ cup

Adobo is a seasoning made from dried chiles, herbs, and spices, and very often includes vinegar. In my version I omit the vinegar, because I usually add it later when I use the adobo as the base for other sauces—this gives me a little more control over the flavor of the finished sauce. The adobo is quick to make: the ingredients are briefly cooked and then all ground together. I recommend making a large batch because it's one of those sauces that the longer it's stored, the better it tastes. It can be refrigerated, tightly covered, for several weeks. The adobo on its own is great for marinating meats, poultry, and fish, and also for rubbing on food before grilling. This recipe can be easily tripled, quadrupled, or even more.

5 dried guajillo chiles
1 tablespoon canola oil
¼ white Spanish onion, sliced
1 small clove garlic
2 whole cloves
3 cinnamon sticks (6 inch), broken into thirds
12 whole black peppercorns
⅛ teaspoon cumin seeds, crushed
1½ cups water

Remove the stems, seeds, and membranes from the chiles. Break the chiles into large pieces and set aside.

In a medium saucepan or skillet, heat the oil over medium-high heat. Add the onion, garlic, cloves, cinnamon, peppercorns, and cumin seeds. Cook, stirring occasionally, until the onion is softened and dark golden brown, about 6 minutes. Add the chiles and cook until darkened on both sides, about 1 minute.

Add the 1½ cups of water—it should cover the ingredients about halfway. Gently boil until reduced by half, 5 to 8 minutes. Scrape into a blender and puree. Pour into a medium-mesh sieve set over a bowl and press the solids with a rubber spatula or the back of a ladle to release the liquid. Discard the solids. Store, tightly covered, in the refrigerator for several weeks.

The Mercado de Toluca (opposite page), in the city of Toluca in the state of Mexico, is typical of the produce markets that are found throughout Mexico.

Pasilla Chile Sauce

Makes about ¾ cup

Similar to the Adobo (see recipe, page 192), this sauce is made with dried pasilla chiles instead of the guajillo chiles called for in the Adobo. The sauce can be drizzled over dishes as a garnish, or used to season soups or the fillings for tacos and tamales. As with similar sauces, you can make big batches and then store it, tightly covered, in the refrigerator for future use.

3 dried pasilla chiles
1 tablespoon canola oil
½ cup chopped white Spanish onion
1 small clove garlic, chopped
1 teaspoon dried marjoram
2 cinnamon sticks, broken
1½ cups water
½ teaspoon salt
⅛ teaspoon freshly ground black pepper

Remove the stems, seeds, and membranes from the chiles. Break the chiles into large pieces and set aside.

In a medium saucepan, heat the oil over medium heat. Add the onion, garlic, marjoram, and cinnamon sticks. Cook, stirring occasionally, until the onion is softened and dark golden brown, about 6 minutes. Add the chiles and cook until darkened on both sides, about 1 minute. Add the 1½ cups water—it should almost cover the ingredients. Gently boil until reduced by a little less than half, 8 to 10 minutes.

Pour into a blender and blend until pureed. Scrape into a medium-mesh sieve placed over a bowl and, using the back of a ladle or a rubber spatula, press the mixture through the sieve. Discard the solids in the sieve. Season the sauce with the salt and pepper. You can store the sauce, tightly covered, in the refrigerator for up to several weeks.

Chile de Arbol Sauce

Makes about 1½ cups

The chile de árbol is a small dried chile that is very hot, but the heavy cream and honey in this sauce temper the heat a bit. The sauce's rosy color makes it an attractive garnish on many of my plates. Drizzle a little of this sauce on tacos for added flavor.

2 dried chiles de árbol
1 tablespoon canola oil
¼ cup chopped white Spanish onion
1 small clove garlic, chopped
1 tablespoon tomato paste
2 tablespoons chopped fresh cilantro leaves
1 cup heavy cream
1 cup Chicken Stock (see recipe, page 186) or canned chicken broth
2 teaspoons honey
½ teaspoon salt
¼ teaspoon freshly ground black pepper

Remove the stems, seeds, and membranes from the chiles, and break the chiles into small pieces. Set aside.

In a medium skillet, heat the oil over medium heat. Add the onion and garlic and sauté for 6 minutes or until the onion is softened—do not let brown. Add the chile pieces and sauté until lightly colored, about 45 seconds. Stir in the tomato paste and cilantro, then the cream, stock, and honey. Gently boil until the sauce is reduced and thickened, 15 to 20 minutes, occasionally scraping the bottom of the pan with a rubber spatula to prevent scorching.

Pour the mixture into a blender and puree. Season with the salt and pepper. The sauce can be stored, tightly covered, in the refrigerator for up to 3 days.

Guajillo Chile Sauce

Makes about ¾ cup

This is another addition to the collection of delicious chile sauces. It is similar to the Adobo (see recipe, page 192) and the Pasilla Chile Sauce (see recipe, left). A bit of it adds great taste to my Pulpo en su Tinta (see recipe, page 95). As with most other sauces, I recommend making a large batch because it will improve the longer it sits. It can be stored in the refrigerator, tightly covered, for several weeks.

5 dried guajillo chiles
1 tablespoon canola oil
½ cup chopped white Spanish onion
1 clove garlic, chopped
1 teaspoon dried marjoram
2 cinnamon sticks, broken into pieces
1½ cups water
1 tablespoon freshly squeezed lemon juice
1 to 2 teaspoons honey, depending on the hotness of the chiles
½ teaspoon salt
⅛ teaspoon freshly ground black pepper

Remove the stems, seeds, and membranes from the chiles. Break the chiles into large pieces and set aside.

In a medium saucepan, heat the oil over medium heat. Add the onion, garlic, and marjoram. Cook, stirring occasionally, until the onion is softened and dark golden brown, about 6 minutes. Add the chiles and the cinnamon sticks and cook, pressing against the bottom of the saucepan with a spatula, until the chile pieces are darkened on both sides, about 1 minute total. Add the 1½ cups water and the lemon juice—the liquid should almost cover the ingredients. Gently boil until reduced by a little less than half, 8 to 10 minutes.

Pour into a blender and blend until pureed. Scrape into a medium-mesh sieve placed over a bowl and, using the back of a ladle or a rubber spatula, press the mixture through the sieve. Discard the solids in the sieve. Season the sauce with the honey, salt, and pepper. Store the sauce, tightly covered, in the refrigerator for several weeks.

Chile de Arbol– Sesame Seed Sauce

Makes about 1 cup

I spoon a little of this sauce on my Tacos de Atún (see recipe, page 82), but it also goes well with salmon or scallops, or stir-fried vegetables such as zucchini, squash, or eggplant.

¼ cup white sesame seeds
2 dried chiles de árbol, stems, seeds, and membranes removed
1 tomato, chopped
¼ cup chopped white Spanish onion
1 tablespoon freshly squeezed lemon juice
1 to 2 tablespoons honey, depending on the hotness of the chiles
¼ teaspoon salt
⅛ teaspoon freshly ground black pepper

Heat a small, dry skillet over medium heat. Add the sesame seeds and toast, shaking the pan occasionally, until lightly colored, about 1 minute—stand back, since some of the seeds will pop. Transfer the seeds to a plate.

In the same skillet, toast the chiles until lightly colored, turning over once, 30 to 45 seconds.

In a blender, combine the tomato, onion, lemon juice, honey, salt, pepper, sesame seeds, and chiles. Puree until smooth. Store in the refrigerator, tightly covered, for up to 3 days.

Sweet Chipotle Sauce

Makes about 2 cups

American barbecue sauces are probably descendant from this tangy sweet sauce, which gets its heat from chipotle chiles. I use it in my Tamal al Chipotle (see recipe, page 66). You can also spoon it over a plain grilled chicken breast or grilled pork, or use it to season taco fillings, such as bean, chicken, fish, or pork.

1 tablespoon canola oil
½ cup chopped white Spanish onion
2 cloves garlic, chopped
1 to 2 canned chipotle chiles in adobo sauce
½ cup freshly squeezed orange juice
½ cup sherry-wine vinegar
½ cup tomato paste
½ cup ketchup
2 to 3 tablespoons honey
½ teaspoon salt
¼ teaspoon freshly ground black pepper

In a large skillet, heat the oil. Add the onion and garlic. Cover and cook or sweat over medium heat until tender, 3 to 5 minutes. Stir in the remaining ingredients and simmer, covered, for 20 minutes. Working in batches, spoon into a blender or small food processor and puree. Strain through a medium-mesh sieve placed over a small bowl, forcing the mixture through with the back of a ladle or a rubber spatula. Store, tightly covered, in the refrigerator for up to a week.

Spicy Tomato Sauce

Makes about 2 cups

I drizzle this uncooked puree over dishes for a garnish, as in my Quesadillas Surtidas (see recipe, page 108).

2 tomatoes, cored and chopped
1 small white Spanish onion, chopped
2 fresh serrano chiles, stemmed, seeded, and chopped
1 teaspoon chopped garlic
1 tablespoon chopped fresh cilantro leaves
½ teaspoon salt
¼ teaspoon freshly ground black pepper
1 teaspoon freshly squeezed lemon juice

Place all the ingredients in a blender and puree until smooth. Store, tightly covered, in the refrigerator for up to 3 days.

Sweet Tomatillo Sauce

Makes about 1 cup

There's no cooking required for this very fresh sauce—everything is just tossed into the blender. It's the topping for my Carnitas de Pato (pictured, below; see recipe, page 101), and it also goes well with chicken and strongly flavored fish such as tuna. And then there are always tortilla chips for a quick accompaniment.

6 fresh tomatillos (pictured, opposite page)
1 to 2 fresh serrano chiles, stemmed and seeded
½ cup chopped fresh cilantro leaves
4 scallions, trimmed and chopped
2 teaspoons honey
½ teaspoon salt
¼ teaspoon freshly ground black pepper

Remove the papery outer husks from the tomatillos, and then rinse the tomatillos to remove any stickiness. Cut into quarters. In a blender, combine the tomatillos and the chiles, and puree. Add the cilantro and scallions, and puree. Add the honey, salt, and pepper, adjusting the honey depending on the hotness of the serrano. Store the sauce, tightly covered, in the refrigerator for up to 2 days, although this sauce is best when first made.

Tomatillo Sauce

Makes about 2 cups

Unlike the Sweet Tomatillo Sauce (see recipe, left), the tomatillos and onion for this sauce are first sautéed for a more mellow flavor. In my Chilaquiles (see recipe, page 146), I mix this sauce with a little heavy cream, and then toss in the tortilla chips. The Tomatillo Sauce is also great for quesadillas or other finger foods, as well as being a wonderful side sauce for practically any dish, such as grilled fish or pork.

1 pound fresh tomatillos
1 tablespoon canola oil, and more as needed
½ cup chopped white Spanish onion
1 large clove garlic, coarsely chopped
2 fresh serrano chiles, seeded and chopped
¼ teaspoon salt
⅛ teaspoon freshly ground black pepper
1 tablespoon chopped fresh cilantro leaves
1 to 2 tablespoons honey (optional; see Note)

Remove the papery husks from the tomatillos. Rinse the tomatillos well to remove any stickiness.

In a large skillet, heat the oil over medium-high heat. Add the tomatillos and onion, and sauté until lightly browned and softened, about 10 minutes. Add the garlic, chiles, salt, and pepper, and sauté until the garlic is lightly browned, about 2 minutes. Remove the skillet from the heat.

Spoon the tomatillo mixture into a blender along with the cilantro. Blend until pureed. Pour into a bowl. Season with salt and pepper, if needed. This sauce can be stored, tightly covered, in the refrigerator for up to 3 days.

Note Depending on the sourness or bitterness of the tomatillos, you may want to add 1 to 2 tablespoons honey to the sauce.

Roasted Red Bell Pepper Sauce

Makes about ½ cup

This makes a flavorful as well as a colorful garnish, and it is especially good drizzled over soups.

1 red bell pepper
3 tablespoons heavy cream
¼ teaspoon salt
⅛ teaspoon freshly ground black pepper

Preheat the broiler. Cut the pepper in half lengthwise. Remove the stem, seeds, and membranes, and discard. Place the halves, cut side down, on a foil-lined baking sheet. Broil 4 inches from the heat until evenly blackened, about 5 minutes. Transfer to a paper bag, seal, and let stand for 10 minutes.

Remove the pepper from the bag, and remove the skin from the pepper halves. Cut the pepper into small pieces. Place in a blender and process until pureed. Add the cream, salt, and black pepper, and puree. Store, tightly covered, in the refrigerator for up to 3 days.

Cilantro Pesto

Makes about ¾ cup

Like a basil-based pesto, this sauce is delicious with chicken or shrimp, or as a marinade for grilling poultry. I sometimes even use it as a sandwich spread.

1 tablespoon canola oil, plus ¼ cup
½ cup chopped white Spanish onion
½ cup packed fresh cilantro leaves, chopped

¼ cup packed snipped fresh chives
¼ cup pine nuts, toasted
1 fresh serrano chile, stemmed, seeded, and chopped
½ teaspoon Roasted Garlic Puree (see recipe, page 205)
2 tablespoons sherry-wine vinegar
2 teaspoons freshly squeezed lemon juice
1 to 2 teaspoons honey, depending on hotness of serrano chile
½ teaspoon salt
⅛ teaspoon freshly ground white pepper
1 tablespoon grated cotija cheese or Parmesan cheese
¼ cup olive oil

In a small skillet, heat the 1 tablespoon canola oil over medium-high heat. Add the onion and sauté until tender and browned, 3 to 4 minutes. Scrape into a blender.

To the blender, add the cilantro, chives, pine nuts, chile, Roasted Garlic Puree, sherry-wine vinegar, lemon juice, honey, salt, white pepper, and cotija cheese. Blend until pureed. Mix together the ¼ cup canola oil and ¼ cup olive oil in a measuring cup. With the blender running, gradually add the oil in a thin stream until well blended and the oil is thoroughly incorporated. Store, tightly covered, in the refrigerator for up to 3 days.

Mole Poblano

Makes about 3 cups

This mole, rich with chocolate, goes well with chicken, pork, beef (see Tampiqueña, page 159), and duck. The three different chiles create the complex heat.

¼ cup unsalted peanuts

¼ cup whole blanched almonds

¼ cup pecans

5 animal crackers

1 tablespoon white sesame seeds

Canola oil, for frying

1 small yellow-black plantain, soft to the touch, peeled, and cut into large cubes

2 dried pasilla chiles

2 dried mulato chiles

2 dried ancho chiles

1 cinnamon stick, broken into pieces

2 whole cloves

¼ teaspoon ground cumin

½ teaspoon salt

¼ teaspoon freshly ground black pepper

2 cups Chicken Stock (see recipe, page 186) or canned chicken broth

¼ cup lard or solid vegetable shortening

⅓ cup (about 1½ ounces) chopped good-quality bittersweet chocolate

Preheat the oven to 350°F. Spread the peanuts, almonds, and pecans on a jelly-roll pan. Toast in the oven, shaking the pan occasionally, until the nuts are slightly colored and fragrant, 3 to 5 minutes. Transfer to a plate. Toast the animal crackers in the oven, for about 3 minutes. Transfer to the plate. In a small, dry skillet, toast the sesame seeds over medium heat, shaking the pan frequently, about 1 minute—be careful, since some of the seeds may pop. Transfer to the plate.

In a deep, medium saucepan, heat about 4 inches of the oil over medium-high heat until it registers 365°F. on a deep-fat frying thermometer. Add the plantain pieces and fry until lightly browned and slightly crisped on the outside, about 3 minutes. With a slotted spoon, transfer the plantain pieces to paper towels to drain. Let oil cool.

Clean the dried chiles, removing the stems, seeds, and membranes. In a dry medium saucepan, toast the chiles over medium-high heat, pressing them against the bottom of the pan with a spatula, until slightly

colored, 30 to 45 seconds per side. Add enough water to almost cover the chiles. Bring to a boil and cook until the chiles are softened, about 5 minutes. Pour into a blender along with the cinnamon stick, cloves, cumin, salt, and pepper. Puree until smooth. Pour into a bowl.

Place the toasted nuts and sesame seeds in the blender. Pour in a little of the stock and puree until the nuts are finely ground, adding a little more stock as needed. Add the animal crackers and plantain pieces, and puree. Pour the nut mixture into the chile mixture. Pour through a medium-mesh sieve placed over a large bowl, pressing on the solids with the back of a ladle or a rubber spatula. Discard the solids in the sieve.

In a medium saucepan, heat the lard. Add the strained liquid along with the remaining stock, stirring to blend. Simmer until thickened to the consistency of a thick pea soup, about 30 minutes, scraping the bottom of the pan frequently with a rubber spatula.

Stir in the chocolate and heat over low heat, stirring, until melted and smooth. Adjust the consistency with stock, if needed. The mole can be stored, tightly covered, in the refrigerator for up to 1 week. To use the mole, gently reheat in a saucepan.

Mole Blanco

White Chocolate Mole

Makes about 1½ cups

The intense dark chocolate mole is an important sauce in many of my dishes, but there are occasions when I want a more subtle flavor. For those dishes, I have created this white chocolate mole, which I spoon around a rack of lamb (see recipe, page 162).

½ cup unsalted peanuts

¼ cup sliced blanched almonds

¼ cup walnuts

2 cups water

1 cinnamon stick, broken into pieces

2 whole cloves

1 fresh poblano chile, cored, seeded, and chopped

2 fresh serrano chiles, cored, seeded, and chopped

1 small clove garlic

½ white Spanish onion, cut into chunks

5 animal crackers, toasted

¼ cup (½ stick) unsalted butter

½ cup chopped white chocolate

½ teaspoon salt

⅛ teaspoon freshly ground white pepper

Glazed earthenware pots and vessels (opposite page) are used extensively in Mexican cooking to create such dishes as moles and pozoles, and atole, a hot chocolate drink.

Preheat the oven to 350°F. Spread the peanuts, almonds, and walnuts on a jelly-roll pan. Toast in the oven, shaking the pan occasionally, until the nuts are slightly colored and fragrant, 3 to 5 minutes. In a blender, combine the nuts, the water, cinnamon stick, and cloves, and blend until the nuts are very finely ground. Strain through a medium-mesh sieve placed over a bowl, pressing on the solids with the back of a ladle or a rubber spatula to release the liquid. Reserve the liquid and discard the solids.

In the blender, combine the chiles, garlic, and onion, and nut liquid. Add the animal crackers and puree. Strain through a medium-mesh sieve set over a bowl, pressing on the solids with the back of a ladle or a rubber spatula to release the liquid. Discard the solids.

In a large saucepan, heat the butter. Stir in the nut-chile liquid. Simmer, uncovered, over medium heat, scraping the bottom of the pan occasionally with a rubber spatula, until the mixture is the consistency of a thick pea soup, about 15 minutes.

Stir in the chocolate and the salt and pepper until the chocolate is melted. Use immediately. The mole without the chocolate can be made ahead and refrigerated, tightly covered, for up to 1 week. To serve, heat in a saucepan and stir in the chocolate.

Pipian Sauce

Pumpkin Seed Sauce

Makes about 4 cups

Toasting the pumpkin seeds and the nuts adds a rich flavor to this sauce. Depending on how hot the serrano chile is, you may want to vary the amount of honey to temper the spiciness of the chile. This is the sauce for my Pipian de Puerco (see recipe, page 155).

1 tablespoon lard or solid vegetable shortening
½ cup chopped white Spanish onion
14 fresh tomatillos, papery husks removed, well rinsed
1 clove garlic
1 large fresh serrano chile
3 cups Chicken Stock (see recipe, page 186) or canned chicken broth
½ cup hulled, unsalted pumpkin seeds, toasted
¼ cup unsalted peanuts, toasted
¼ cup pecans, toasted
¼ cup sliced almonds, toasted
1 cup fresh cilantro leaves
1½ teaspoons sherry-wine vinegar
½ teaspoon honey
½ teaspoon salt
⅛ teaspoon freshly ground white pepper

In a medium saucepan, heat the lard. Add the onion, tomatillos, garlic, and chile, and sauté, stirring occasionally, for 10 minutes, or until lightly browned and softened. Add the stock, pumpkin seeds, and all the nuts. Bring to a boil, then lower the heat and very gently simmer, uncovered, over very low heat for 30 minutes, stirring occasionally—the pumpkin seeds and nuts should be softened and the mixture should be very soupy.

Working in batches if necessary, pour the mixture into a blender and add the cilantro. Puree until smooth. Season with the vinegar, honey, salt, and pepper. Store, tightly covered, in the refrigerator for up to 3 days. (The cilantro will begin to darken after about an hour.)

Chile de Arbol– Tomato Seed Vinaigrette

Makes about 1⅔ cups

For the guacamole in the restaurant, we use lots of tomatoes, which we first seed and juice. Rather than throwing out all that good liquid, I created this recipe to incorporate the seeds and juice into a dressing. I use it as a garnish for Langosta y Camarones (see recipe, page 140).

2 pounds ripe tomatoes
1 to 2 dried chiles de árbol, stemmed, seeded, and broken into pieces
1 tablespoon sherry-wine vinegar
1 tablespoon freshly squeezed lime juice
½ to ¾ cup canola oil
2 to 3 teaspoons honey
¼ teaspoon salt
⅛ teaspoon freshly ground black pepper

Cut the tomatoes in half. Working over a bowl, use the tips of your fingers to scoop out the juice and seeds from the tomato cavities into the bowl—you should have about 1 cup. Refrigerate the remaining tomato flesh for guacamole, salads, or soups.

In a blender, process the tomato juice and seeds, the chiles, vinegar, and lime juice. With the blender running, slowly add the oil in a thin stream until it is emulsified or thoroughly incorporated. Blend in the honey, salt, and pepper. Adjust the seasonings, if necessary. Refrigerate, covered, for up to 3 days.

Chipotle Rouille

Makes about 1 cup

A French sauce made with chiles and olive oil, rouille is used to garnish bouillabaisse, the classic fish stew from Provence. This recipe is an excellent example of how I like to work the flavors of other cuisines into my style of Mexican cooking. The rouille also makes a great dressing for coleslaw. I've discovered an interesting flavor variation by substituting Vietnamese or Thai chile sauce for the chipotles in adobo.

2 canned chipotle chiles in adobo
1 cup canola oil
2 large egg yolks
1 tablespoon freshly squeezed lemon juice
½ teaspoon salt
¼ teaspoon freshly ground white pepper
Honey, to taste

In a blender, process the chiles and oil until pureed.

In a medium bowl, using an electric mixer with a whisk attachment or whisking by hand, beat the egg yolks until thick and lemon-colored. Drop by drop, whisk in the oil mixture—don't rush, or the oil may separate from the yolks. Once the mixture begins to thicken, slowly add the oil in a thin steady stream, stopping the stream frequently to make sure the oil is being absorbed. Season with the lemon juice, salt, white pepper, and honey to taste. Refrigerate, covered, for up to 3 days.

Bottled Mayonnaise Variation Place 1 cup bottled mayonnaise in a bowl. In a blender, puree the chipotle chiles. Stir into the mayonnaise. Season with the lemon juice, salt, pepper, and honey to taste.

Chive-Habanero Rouille Omit the chipotle chiles in adobo in the above recipe. In a blender, puree together 1 cup snipped fresh chives, 1 fresh habanero chile, stemmed and seeded, and the canola oil. Proceed with the rest of the recipe. For a bottled mayonnaise variation, finely chop the chives and chile, and stir into the mayonnaise.

Tamarind Vinaigrette

Makes about ½ cup

I often use the vinaigrette as a marinade for pork (see Pipian de Puerco, page 155) and duck. But my real favorite is drizzling the vinaigrette over a grilled chicken salad.

2 tablespoons tamarind paste (See Note, below)
2 tablespoons sherry-wine vinegar
2 teaspoons honey
¼ teaspoon salt
⅛ teaspoon freshly ground black pepper
½ cup canola oil

In a small bowl, mash together the tamarind paste and the vinegar with a fork until smooth. Scrape into a sieve placed over a bowl, and press through with a rubber spatula. Discard the solids in the sieve. Into the tamarind mixture in the bowl, stir the honey, salt, and pepper. Slowly whisk in the oil in a thin stream until fully incorporated and the dressing is thick. Store, tightly covered, in the refrigerator for up to 1 week.

Chipotle-Tamarind Vinaigrette When preparing the vinaigrette following the recipe above, add 1 canned chipotle in adobo, seeded and chopped, to the tamarind-vinegar mixture when mashing together. Then proceed with the rest of the recipe.

Note You can substitute 2 teaspoons tamarind concentrate for the tamarind paste. In a small bowl, whisk together the concentrate and the vinegar. Then whisk in the honey, salt, and pepper, and proceed with the rest of the recipe.

Citrus Vinaigrette

Makes about 2 cups

In addition to dressing salads with this vinaigrette, I like to serve it with steamed artichokes, and I also drizzle a little bit over cooked fish instead of the usual lemon juice.

1 cup freshly squeezed orange juice
¼ cup freshly squeezed lemon juice
¼ cup distilled white vinegar
2 teaspoons honey
½ cup canola oil
½ teaspoon salt
¼ teaspoon freshly ground black pepper

In a small saucepan, boil the orange juice until reduced to about ⅔ cup. Let cool.

In a blender, combine the orange juice, lemon juice, vinegar, and honey. Process until blended. With the motor running, slowly add the oil until well blended and the mixture is thickened. Season with the salt and pepper. Store, tightly covered, in the refrigerator for up to 3 days.

Tomato Vinaigrette

Make about 2 cups

This is a hearty vinaigrette that pairs well with strongly flavored greens. It is also delicious spooned over salads made with cooked chicken, pork, salmon, and tuna.

2 tomatoes, cored and chopped
2 tablespoons sherry-wine vinegar
1 teaspoon honey
¼ teaspoon salt
⅛ teaspoon freshly ground black pepper
¼ cup canola oil

In a blender or small food processor, combine the tomato, vinegar, honey, salt, and pepper. Blend until pureed. With the motor running, gradually add the oil until well blended. Taste and adjust the seasoning with additional vinegar, honey, salt, and pepper, if needed. Store, tightly covered, in the refrigerator for up to 3 days.

Roasted Tomato Vinaigrette

Makes about 2 cups

In addition to using the vinaigrette as a salad dressing, I like to marinate fish in this sauce before grilling it. The dressing is a delicious accent for chicken dishes and is a colorful garnish when drizzled over soups.

2 tomatoes, cored, halved, seeded, and halves quartered
4 cloves garlic, peeled
1 dried pasilla chile
2 teaspoons honey, or to taste
½ teaspoon salt
¼ teaspoon freshly ground black pepper
1 cup canola oil

Preheat the oven to 400°F. Place the tomatoes and garlic on a jelly-roll pan. Roast for 20 minutes or until the skins are wrinkled. Set aside.

Split the chile in half lengthwise. Remove the stem, seeds, and membanes. Heat a small, dry skillet over medium heat. Spread the chile open and place it in the skillet, pressing it flat with a spatula. Toast for 15 to 30 seconds. Then flip over and toast the other side. Set aside.

In a blender, combine the tomatoes, garlic, chile, honey, salt, and pepper. Blend until pureed. With the blender running, slowly add the oil in a thin stream until it is fully incorporated into the vinaigrette. Store, tightly covered, in the refrigerator for up to 3 days.

Huitlacoche Vinaigrette

Make about 1½ cups

Huitlacoche is a fungus that grows on corn. I like to use this vinaigrette with dishes that are a little bland so the subtle flavor of the huitlacoche is not over-powered. For example, a drizzle of the vinaigrette is perfect with pan-seared fresh tuna. In my Halibut con Pepitas (see recipe, page 131) I flavor the mashed potatoes with huitlacoche, and in Pescado al Chipotle (see recipe, page 130) I season the rice with huitla-coche. To learn more about huitlacoche, see Notes on Ingredients (page 26).

3 teaspoons huitlacoche
1 teaspoon honey
¼ cup sherry-wine vinegar
½ teaspoon salt
¼ teaspoon freshly ground black pepper
1 cup canola oil

In a small bowl, mix the huitlacoche, honey, vinegar, salt, and pepper. Slowly whisk in the oil. Store, tightly covered, in the refrigerator for up to 2 days.

Guacamole

Makes about 3½ cups

Guacamole is probably the most popular side dish served in Mexico, and it's wonderful because it goes well with just about anything. For the best results, pre-pare the guacamole just prior to serving.

4 Haas avocados (about 2½ pounds)
½ cup diced (¼ inch), seeded tomato
¼ cup diced (¼ inch) white Spanish onion
2 fresh serrano chiles, stemmed, seeded, deveined, and diced
2 tablespoons thin strips of fresh cilantro
¼ teaspoon salt
2 teaspoons freshly squeezed lemon juice, or to taste

Halve the avocados and remove the pits. Scoop the meat into a bowl. Add the remaining ingredients and mix well. Taste and adjust the seasoning with salt and lemon juice, and more chiles, if desired.

At Roberto Romo's ranch in Taxco, guacamole and chips are served in the same manner as they are at Maya (opposite page): a three-legged molcajete, made from volcanic rock, holds the chips, and the guacamole is piled in a silver bowl crafted by the silversmiths who work at Romo's ranch. The blue-rimmed glasses are typical of the handblow glass from the town of Tonalá.

becomes speckled, another 30 seconds or so. The tortilla may puff a little. Transfer to a clean kitchen towel and cover to keep warm. Repeat with the remaining dough, cooking a couple of tortillas at a time if possible.

As you take the tortillas off the griddle, stack them in the clean kitchen towel, keeping the tortillas covered.

Corn Tortillas

Makes about 16 tortillas

Corn tortillas are a staple in the cuisine of Mexico, in the same way that bread is in another cultures. Tortillas, in fact, are a flat bread. We eat them plain for breakfast, lunch, and dinner. But they can also appear in other guises. I use day-old tortillas broken into pieces for Chilaquiles (see recipe, page 146). In the past, to make tortillas you had to first dry the corn kernels, then soak them in a lime solution, and then put them through a mill to produce the masa or flour to make the tortillas. Things have changed in the last fifteen years. Now we have a corn flour specifically produced for tortilla-making. All you do is add water and knead. (See photos, opposite page.)

2 cups instant corn masa mix for tortillas
1 cup plus 2 tablespoons tepid water

In a medium bowl, mix together the masa and tepid water. Knead in the bowl until a soft dough forms—if too dry, add a little more water; or if too wet, add a little more masa mix.

Shape the dough into 16 small balls, about 1 ounce of dough each, and cover with a kitchen towel.

Heat a griddle or heavy cast-iron skillet over medium heat, using two burners if necessary. Keep one part of the surface a little cooler than the rest.

Meanwhile, lay a piece of plastic wrap or waxed paper on the bottom plate of a tortilla press. Place a ball of dough in the center, and lay a piece of plastic wrap or paper on top of the ball. Lift over the top plate and press the ball into a circle. Raise the top plate and peel off the top piece of wrap—the tortilla should be about 5 to 6 inches in diameter and about 1/8 inch thick. Invert the tortilla onto the fingers of one hand and then carefully peel off the second piece of wrap. Lay the tortilla on the cooler part of the griddle, sweeping your hand out of the way. Let the tortilla sit until it releases from the griddle, 10 to 15 seconds. Carefully using your fingers or a spatula, flip the tortilla over onto the hotter part of the griddle and let it cook until the bottom begins to speckle with brown spots, 30 to 40 seconds. Flip the tortilla over and let it cook until the bottom side

Corn Tortilla Chips

Makes 4 servings

When I first moved to the United States, I discovered that one of the biggest myths in this country about Mexico was that all Mexicans eat tortilla chips and salsa. But now tortilla chips are actually one of my favorite finger foods. Homemade chips are the best, and they're even better if you make your own salsa and guacamole to go with them.

Canola oil, for frying
6 yellow or blue corn tortillas (10 inch),
**   each cut into 8 triangles**
Salt, to taste

In a deep saucepan, heat 2 to 3 inches of canola oil over medium heat until it registers 350°F. on a deep-fat frying thermometer. Working in batches, add the tortilla triangles and fry until crisp and light brown, about 1 minute. With a slotted spoon, transfer them to a large roasting pan or baking sheet lined with paper towels. Sprinkle with salt to season.

Crisp Tortilla Strips Cut a corn tortilla into very thin strips, about 1/8 inch wide. Fry as above, but only for about 30 seconds.

Garlic Mashed Potatoes

Makes 4 servings

The Roasted Garlic Puree is what makes these potatoes special—the roasting sweetens and deepens the flavor of the garlic. The potatoes stand up very well to the balsamic vinegar sauce and the chorizo-stuffed pork chop in my Chuleta de Puerco en Vinagre Balsamico (see recipe, page 152). The huitlacoche version which follows has a complex flavor that nicely complements the pumpkin seeds in my Halibut con Pepitas (see recipe, page 131).

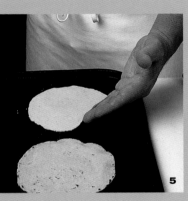

1 Roll the tortilla dough into walnut-size balls, about 1¼ to 1½ inches in diameter. **2** Lay a round piece of plastic wrap or waxed paper on the bottom plate of a tortilla press, and place a ball of dough in the center. **3** Place a piece of plastic wrap on top of the ball. Lower the top plate and press the ball of dough into a circle. Lift the top plate, then peel off the top piece of plastic wrap from the tortilla. **4** Invert the tortilla onto the fingers of one hand and carefully peel off the second piece of plastic wrap. **5** Lay the tortilla on the griddle, sweeping your hand out of the way. Cook according to the recipe (opposite page), until the tortillas are speckled with small brown spots.

3 boiling potatoes (about 1 pound)
1½ teaspoons salt
½ cup half-and-half
¼ cup (½ stick) butter
1 teaspoon Roasted Garlic Puree (see recipe, right)
Pinch freshly ground black pepper

Peel the potatoes and cut into chunks. Place in a large saucepan and cover with cold water. Bring to a boil. Add 1 teaspoon of the salt and boil until tender, about 20 minutes.

Meanwhile, in a small saucepan, heat together the half-and-half and butter.

Drain the potatoes and return to the pan and mash. Stir in the hot half-and-half mixture, the Roasted Garlic Puree, the remaining ½ teaspoon salt, and the pepper.

Huitlacoche Mashed Potatoes In a small bowl, mash ¼ cup huitlacoche with a fork. Substitute the huitlacoche for the Roasted Garlic Puree in the recipe above.

Roasted Garlic Puree

Makes about 2 tablespoons

It's always nice to have a little of this puree on hand for flavoring vegetables, sauces, and fillings for tacos and tamales. The garlic becomes sweeter as it roasts.

12 cloves garlic, papery skin removed but unpeeled
2 tablespoons canola oil

Preheat the oven to 300°F. In a small baking dish, mix together the garlic and oil to coat the garlic. Roast until the garlic is soft, about 40 minutes. Remove from the oven.

When cool enough to handle, cut off the hard end of the cloves, and squeeze the garlic out of the skin into a small bowl. Mash to a puree with a fork. Store the puree, tightly covered, in the refrigerator for up to 3 days.

Potato Crisps

Makes 4 crisps

These lacy potato pancakes or crisps make a crunchy accompaniment to most eggs dishes. I also sandwich them in my Salmón Maya (see recipe, page 113).

2 Yukon Gold potatoes or other boiling potatoes
Canola oil, for frying
½ teaspoon salt
¼ teaspoon freshly ground black pepper

Preheat the oven to 250°F.

Peel the potatoes and cut each in half. Thinly shred the potato halves with a mandoline or a grater, keeping each pile separate. On a piece of waxed paper, spread each pile into a thin circle, about 3 inches in diameter.

In a large saucepan, heat about 3 inches of canola oil until it registers 365°F. on a deep-fat frying thermometer. Using a metal spatula, slide one of the potato circles into the hot oil. With tongs or a fork, spread the potato in the oil so it makes a lacy pancake. Cook until lightly golden on the underside, 2 to 3 minutes. With the tongs, gently flip the crisp over and cook for another 2 to 3 minutes, or until golden and crisp on the underside. Transfer to a paper towel–lined baking sheet and keep warm in the oven. Repeat to make 3 more crisps, for a total of 4. Season with the salt and pepper.

Potato and Rajas Gratin

Makes 8 servings

This is an easy side dish that goes well with most grilled meats. The strips of roasted poblano chiles—the rajas—layered with the potato slices add a slightly smoky flavor. The recipe is easily cut in half and baked in a 11 x 7 x 2-inch casserole dish.

4 fresh poblano chiles
2 cups heavy cream
½ teaspoon salt
¼ teaspoon freshly ground white pepper
6 boiling potatoes (2½ to 3 pounds), peeled and sliced ⅛ inch thick
6 ounces goat cheese

Preheat the broiler. Place the chiles on a baking sheet and broil about 4 inches from the heat, turning occasionally, until blackened on all sides, about 20 minutes.

Place the chiles in a brown paper bag and let them stand for 10 minutes. Reduce the oven temperature to 350°F. Remove the chiles from the bag. When cool enough to handle, cut each chile in half, remove the stems, seeds, and membranes, and peel off the skin. Cut the chiles lengthwise into thin strips. Set aside.

In a small saucepan, heat the cream. Season with the salt and pepper.

In the bottom of a 13 x 9 x 2-inch baking dish, layer a quarter of the potato slices. Arrange a third of the poblano strips over the top and sprinkle with a quarter of the goat cheese. Ladle a quarter of the cream over the top. Repeat 3 more potato layers, ending with cheese on top. Cover the dish tightly with aluminum foil. Bake for 1½ hours. Remove from the oven and let stand for 15 minutes before serving.

Potato Gratin For a plain potato gratin with a less assertive flavor, omit the roasted poblano chiles.

Chayote Gratin

Makes 4 servings

I serve a portion of this with my popular Salmón Maya (see recipe, page 113). Since chayote has a somewhat neutral flavor, I bake it in a gratin with goat cheese and cotija cheese. This dish makes a delicious vegetarian lunch or supper when served with a green salad.

1 cup heavy cream
3 tablespoons soft goat cheese
2 chayotes, peeled, halved, pitted, and cut crosswise into ⅛-inch-thick slices
½ teaspoon salt
¼ teaspoon freshly ground white pepper
½ cup grated cotija cheese or Parmesan cheese

Preheat the oven to 350°F. In a small saucepan, heat together the cream and goat cheese over low heat, stirring, until the cheese is melted.

In a 9-inch glass pie plate, layer the chayote slices, seasoning each layer with the salt and white pepper. Ladle in the warm cream mixture. Sprinkle the cotija cheese over the top. Cover the pie plate with aluminum foil.

Bake for 60 minutes, until the chayote is tender. Remove the aluminum foil and continue to bake until the top is browned, about 15 minutes. Let stand for 30 minutes before serving.

Chocolate Sauce

Makes about 1 cup

I have always liked chocolate sauce on the warm side, so if you make this ahead, I recommend that you gently warm it in a saucepan over low heat, or briefly microwave it.

1 cup coarsely chopped good-quality bittersweet chocolate
¾ cup milk
1 tablespoon sugar
1 cinnamon stick, broken into pieces

In the top of a double boiler, heat the chocolate over gently simmering water until it melts. Stir until smooth.

Meanwhile, in a medium saucepan, stir together the milk, sugar, and cinnamon stick pieces. Heat over medium heat until bubbles appear around the edge of the pan.

Remove the cinnamon stick pieces from the milk. Remove the top of the double boiler with the melted chocolate from over the water. Gradually stir the milk mixture into the chocolate until well blended. Strain through a fine-mesh sieve over a small bowl. Serve warm, or refrigerate, tightly covered, for up to 1 week.

Guava Sauce

Makes about 2 cups

Sweet-tart, this sauce is a flavorful garnish for practically any dessert, including plain ice cream. The fruit is in season from October to December.

2 cups diced, peeled guava (3 to 4)
1 cup water
½ cup sugar

In a medium saucepan, stir together the diced guava, the water, and sugar. Bring to a boil. Pour into a blender and puree until smooth. Pour through a medium-mesh sieve place over a bowl, pressing through with a rubber spatula. Store, tightly covered, in the refrigerator for up to a week.

Strawberry Sauce

Makes about 2 cups

This fruit sauce and the two that follow, which I use to garnish many of my desserts at the restaurant, are simple to make and add a special difference to the flavor and presentation of the desserts. They're nice to have on hand and keep well in the refrigerator for up to a week, so they can be drizzled over ice cream or flavored yogurts at a moment's notice. Experiment with other fruits for different colors and tastes.

2 cups fresh strawberries, rinsed and hulled
1 cup water
½ cup sugar

In a medium saucepan, stir together the strawberries, the water, and sugar. Bring to a boil. Pour into a blender and puree until smooth. Pour through a medium-mesh sieve placed over a bowl, pressing through with a rubber spatula. Discard the solids. Store, tightly covered, in the refrigerator for up to 1 week.

Raspberry Sauce

Makes about 2 cups

2 cups fresh raspberries
1 cup water
1 cup sugar

In a medium saucepan, stir together the raspberries, the water, and sugar. Bring to a boil. Pour into a blender and puree until smooth. Pour through a medium-mesh sieve placed over a bowl, pressing through with a rubber spatula. Discard the seeds. Store, tightly covered, in the refrigerator for up to 1 week.

Blackberry Sauce

Makes about 2 cups

2 cups fresh blackberries
1 cup water
½ cup sugar

In a medium saucepan, stir together the blackberries, the water, and sugar. Bring to a boil. Pour into a blender and puree until smooth. Pour through a medium-mesh sieve placed over a bowl, pressing through with a rubber spatula. Discard the seeds. Store, tightly covered, in the refrigerator for up to 1 week.

Vanilla Sauce

Makes about 1 cup

This all-purpose dessert sauce goes with practically anything, even plain pieces of cake or cut-up fresh fruit.

1 cup milk
2 teaspoons sugar
2 large egg yolks

In a small saucepan, boil together the milk and sugar, stirring until the sugar is dissolved. In a small bowl, lightly beat the egg yolks. Stir in a little of the hot milk mixture. Stir the yolk mixture into the milk mixture in the saucepan. Over very low heat, cook, stirring, until thick enough to coat the back of a spoon, 1 to 2 minutes—be careful not to let mixture boil or the sauce will curdle. Pour through a fine-mesh sieve placed over a bowl, gently forcing the sauce through with a rubber spatula. Let cool, and then refrigerate to chill. Store, tightly covered, in the refrigerator for up to 3 days.

Caramel Sauce

Makes about ½ cup

A drizzle or a few drops of this sauce add a glistening touch, as well as a sweet accent to a dessert plate.

½ cup sugar
¼ cup water

In a small skillet, stir together the sugar and water. Bring to a boil, stirring to dissolve the sugar, and continue to gently boil, without stirring, until amber, about 5 minutes. To store, let cool and pour into a clean glass container. To use, gently reheat.

Candied Walnuts

Makes about 1 cup

You might wonder why chefs go to the trouble of making different garnishes for desserts. For me, desserts are just as important as entrées, and all the elements of the dessert should harmonize and contribute to the final experience. For example, candied walnuts provide texture and sweetness. In a dessert such as Crepas de Cajeta (see recipe, page 179) in which the crepes and bananas are soft, the walnuts add the note of crunchy contrast. The same would be true for a fruit mousse—

the sweetness and crunch of the walnuts nicely balances the smoothness and slight acidity of the mousse. Creating a dish is always about balance.

2 large egg whites
½ cup granulated sugar
1 cup shelled walnuts (about 4 ounces)

Preheat the oven to 350°F. In a shallow bowl, lightly beat the egg whites to break them up. Spread the sugar on a sheet of waxed paper. Very lightly coat each walnut with egg white, roll in sugar to lightly coat, and place on a baking sheet.

Bake until the sugar has melted and turned golden, 8 to 10 minutes. Remove the baking sheet to a wire rack and allow to cool. Store the walnuts in an airtight container at room temperature for up to 1 week.

Crepes

Makes about 12 crepes

½ cup (1 stick) unsalted butter, melted and cooled
3 large eggs
¼ cup milk
¾ cup all-purpose flour
½ cup sugar
Pinch salt
Canola oil

In a blender, combine the butter, eggs, and milk, and pulse the mixture to blend well. Add the flour, sugar, and salt, and puree until smooth. Let stand for 30 minutes to allow the gluten in the flour relax.

Lightly coat an 8-inch nonstick crepe pan or skillet with a little of the canola oil. Heat over medium heat. If the batter has thickened too much, thin with a little more milk until it has a good coating consistency. Add 2 tablespoons of the batter to the pan, swirling the pan so the batter evenly coats the bottom. Cook until both sides are golden, about 1 minute per side—be careful that the crepe doesn't become crisp around the edges. Remove the crepe to a plate. Continue until all the batter is used, coating the pan with oil as needed. Separate the crepes on the plate with sheets of waxed paper. Refrigerate for up to 2 days if not using right away, or wrap tightly and freeze for up to several weeks.

Fruit paste candies (opposite page), including guava and quince, are a popular treat throughout Mexico. They are eaten with the comida, or midday meal, and are often served with coffee after the evening meal.

Tuiles

Makes about 16 tuiles

These are the perfect dessert garnish when I need crunch and a little sweetness. And to make the whole effect even more extravagant, I'll often place a small scoop of ice cream on top of the tuile, as in the Tamal de Chocolate (see recipe, page 170).

½ cup all-purpose flour
6 tablespoons sugar
½ cup (1 stick) unsalted butter, melted
2 large egg whites

In a medium bowl, with an electric mixer, beat together the flour and sugar on low speed just until combined. Increase the speed to medium-low, and gradually add the butter. Continue to beat until combined. Gradually beat in the egg whites until well blended. Remove the bowl from the mixer, and if the batter is not totally blended stir the batter with a rubber spatula. Cover and refrigerate overnight.

Preheat the oven to 350°F. Line a jelly-roll pan with parchment paper, or butter the pan. For each tuile, spoon about 2 teaspoons of the batter onto the paper or pan, spacing about 4 inches apart. Using a butter knife, spread the batter into about 2-inch circles.

Bake until lightly browned, 8 to 10 minutes—the batter will spread into flat cookies. Remove the pan from the oven to a wire rack. Let the tuiles stand for 1 minute. Using a thin metal spatula, remove a tuile, and place it over the bottom of an inverted custard cup, making a slight indentation in the cookie. Repeat with the remaining tuiles, working quickly. The tuiles should harden in about 10 minutes.

Repeat with the remaining batter, using a clean, cool pan each time, either lined with parchment or buttered fresh. Store the tuiles in an airtight container at room temperature for up to 3 days.

Acknowledgments

Here are all the people I want to thank for the important parts they played—both direct and indirect—in helping me write this book.

Marco Colantonio is a dear friend from the early days of Maya New York. And in large part this book is a result of his stubbornness—his pushing me to organize my recipes and to write about Mexico. As long as I've known Marco, he has always been generous with his faith in me. Despite the fact that I haven't always listened to his advice—usually to my regret—he is still willing to share his insights into the complicated world of running a restaurant.

Ignacio Urquiza is the talented photographer responsible for all the beautiful pictures in this book. He shares my love for the spirit of Mexico, and as we traveled through the country photographing haciendas, ranches, people, vistas, and plates of my food, Ignacio always aimed to capture the perfect moment. That often meant spending long days searching for the perfect light and the perfect location.

Laura Cordera and Leticia Alexander are the food stylists who without fail had all the ingredients ready for every food photograph, no matter where we were in Mexico. Mariana Hagerman, with her creativeness and wonderful props, helped to transform my vision of showcasing a modern Mexico into pictures.

David Gonzales is the talented chef of Maya New York. His trusted hand in the kitchen, along with the help of Marcos Lopez, his sous chef, and the rest of the kitchen staff at Maya, made it possible for me to go to Denver to open Tamayo. David was also instrumental in compiling and working through all the recipes for this book.

Luis, Raiza, Zulima, Edwin, and the rest of the great out-front staff of Maya New York have taken care of Maya as if it were their own, ensuring its continued popularity.

Sean Yontz is the chef of Tamayo in Denver, and his understanding of my food, as well as his hard work and dedication to the restaurant, have played a significant role in Tamayo's success. Besides all that, he too spent a great deal of time helping to put together recipes for this book.

The whole staff at Tamayo Denver has helped create a restaurant that quickly earned praise from the press as one of that city's best, and they continue to strive to make it even better.

Morning light reflects off a waterfall on the ranch of Roberto Romo and Emilia Castillo near Taxco, Mexico (opposite page). They are the husband-and-wife artists who designed the interior of Maya New York.

My father, Manuel Sandoval, taught me by his example the importance of good restaurant management. He made me a businessman, and not just a chef. For that, I thank him immensely.

Roberto Romo, an artist and fellow restaurateur, taught me a great deal about the restaurant business. He and his wife, Emilia Castillo, helped me design Maya New York, and I'm still amazed at their creativity in building such a wonderful environment, and with very limited resources.

Paul Casanova, my mother's husband, has encouraged me to follow my instincts, and along with my mother he has helped me attain my goals.

I wish I could say that my mother, Barbara Casanova, has inspired my cooking, but I would be fibbing if I did. But what she has given me is much more important. Even when she didn't necessarily agree with my plans, it was her confidence in my abilities that allowed me to leave Mexico six years ago and head for New York City.

My wife, Gabriela, has continuously supported me and believed in my visions. But most important, she has devoted herself to raising our two children, Giancarlo and Isabella.

My brother, Felipe, who is my partner in Maya San Francisco, chef Aldofo Larreynaga, and the restaurant staff there have continually maintained the quality of Maya SF, allowing me to carry out my other projects.

Antonio Brodziak, my friend and sous chef, helped me open Maya New York and San Francisco.

Leslie Stoker, publisher at Stewart, Tabori & Chang, liked the idea of a book about my cooking from the very beginning, and I'm happy she was willing to take me on as a first-time author.

David Ricketts shared his knowledge about food and making a book, and tested all my recipes, helping to fine-tune them for the home kitchen. He also worked with me in compiling the information that appears in this book.

Susi Oberhelman is the book designer who created these beautiful pages and made sense of the hundreds of photos we took in Mexico.

A special thanks to the following in Mexico: La Casa que Canta hotel in Zihuatanejo; Villa Montaña hotel in Morelia; Monte Xanic vineyards; and Margarita Alvarez.

There is one large group whom I can never thank enough—all the people who dine at my three restaurants. I get a kick out of walking through the dining rooms and seeing people talking and happily eating my food. It's as though I were back at my grandparents' house in Mexico City, enjoying one of our weekend family get-togethers.

And then there is Mexico, the wonderful country where I was born. Its rich culture inspired me to create Maya as a showcase for contemporary Mexican cuisine and crafts.

Food, culture, and art are just a few of the wonderful things about Mexico that will capture your imagination. And a good place to get your feet wet when you begin to explore is La Casa que Canta, overlooking Zihuatanejo Bay along the Pacific coast north of Acapulco.

Ingredient Sources

CHILE TODAY HOT TAMALE

An assortment of dried chiles and chile powders, as well as hot sauces

919 Highway 33, Suite 47
Freehold, NJ 07728
800-468-7377

THE CMC COMPANY

Diverse selection of Mexican ingredients, including dried chiles, achiote paste, Mexican chocolate, and masa harina

P.O. Drawer 222
Avalon, NJ 08202
Tel: 800-262-2780
Fax: 609-861-3065
www.thecmccompany.com

KITCHEN

One stop-shopping: dried chiles, flours, dried corn husks, tamarind, hibiscus, panko, Búfalo sauce, and on and on

218 Eighth Avenue
New York, NY 10011
888-HOT-4433
www.kitchenmarket.com

LE MAJOR FOODS OF MEXICO

Extensive inventory of chiles, tortillas, flours, cajeta de leche, prepared moles, and tortilla presses

www.lamejor.com

The Mercado de San Juan in Mexico City (below) offers a wide variety of quality foodstuffs including tomatoes, potatoes, avocados, and chiles.

Conversion Chart

WEIGHT EQUIVALENTS

The metric weights given in this chart are not exact equivalents, but have been rounded up or down slightly to make measuring easier.

AVOIRDUPOIS	METRIC
¼ oz	7 g
½ oz	15 g
1 oz	30 g
2 oz	60 g
3 oz	90 g
4 oz	115 g
5 oz	150 g
6 oz	175 g
7 oz	200 g
8 oz (½ lb)	225 g
9 oz	250 g
10 oz	300 g
11 oz	325 g
12 oz	350 g
13 oz	375 g
14 oz	400 g
15 oz	425 g
16 oz (1 lb)	450 g
1½ lb	750 g
2 lb	900 g
2¼ lb	1 kg
3 lb	1.4 kg
4 lb	1.8 kg

VOLUME EQUIVALENTS

These are not exact equivalents for American cups and spoons, but have been rounded up or down slightly to make measuring easier.

AMERICAN	METRIC	IMPERIAL
¼ t	1.2 ml	
½ t	2.5 ml	
1 t	5.0 ml	
½ T (1.5 t)	7.5 ml	
1 T (3 t)	15 ml	
¼ cup (4 T)	60 ml	2 fl oz
⅓ cup (5 T)	75 ml	2½ fl oz
½ cup (8 T)	125 ml	4 fl oz
⅔ cup (10 T)	150 ml	5 fl oz
¾ cup (12 T)	175 ml	6 fl oz
1 cup (16 T)	250 ml	8 fl oz
1¼ cups	300 ml	10 fl oz (½ pt)
1½ cups	350 ml	12 fl oz
2 cups (1 pint)	500 ml	16 fl oz
2½ cups	625 ml	20 fl oz (1 pint)
1 quart	1 liter	32 fl oz

OVEN TEMPERATURE EQUIVALENTS

OVEN MARK	F	C	GAS
Very cool	250–275	130–140	½–1
Cool	300	150	2
Warm	325	170	3
Moderate	350	180	4
Moderately hot	375	190	5
	400	200	6
Hot	425	220	7
	450	230	8
Very hot	475	250	9

Index

(Page numbers in *italic* refer to illustrations.)

Mizuna:
> avocado and crabmeat terrine, 88, *89*
> yellow and red tomato salad with manchego cheese and, 48–49, *49*

Mole:
> *blanco, rack de cordero en,* 162
> *de pétalos de rosa, cordero en,* 163
> *poblano, pechuga con,* 145
> *verde, cordero en, 164,* 165

Mole(s), 26, 144
> green, with roasted vegetables, lamb shank in, *164,* 165
> poblano, 199
> poblano, grilled chicken breast with, 145
> rose petal, lamb with, 163
> tamarind, 102–3
> white chocolate *(mole blanco),* 199–200
> white chocolate, rack of lamb with, 162

Mousse, frozen coffee, 183
Mousse de café de olla, 183
Mulato, 23
Mushroom(s):
> adobo, melted manchego cheese with tomatillo sauce and, 109
> chipotle sauce, 130
> dumplings, 128–29
> shiitake, warm spinach salad with, 47
> strudel with sweet potato puree, 166–67, *167*

Mussels:
> grilled cactus and seafood salad with apple–serrano chile vinaigrette, *50,* 51
> sautéed scallops, shrimp, clams and, with roasted garlic puree and black rice, *138,* 139

N

Napoleon, lobster, with creamy goat cheese and arugula salad, 87
Napoleon de langosta, 87
Nogada, chile en, 104, 105
Nogada sauce, veal-stuffed poblano chile with, *104,* 105
Nopal, ensalada de, 50, 51

O

Oaxaca (cheese), 22, *22*
Octopus:
> and mixed shellfish ceviche with sweet-and-spicy tomato broth, 37
> in squid ink with sweet potato pancake and pea shoot salad, 95

Oils:
> canola, 21
> chive, 190
> cilantro, 190
> epazote, 190
> guajillo chile, 190
> lemon, 190
> pasilla chile, 190–91
> *see also* Emulsions

Onions:
> fried, 156–57
> grilled, 158
> marinated, *126,* 127
> seasoned, 75
> white Spanish, 26

Orange:
> watercress, hearts of palm, and avocado with citrus vinaigrette, 44, *45*
> *see also* Blood orange

Ostiones:
> *Fritas,* 80
> *Sandoval,* 78, *79*

Oysters:
> baked, topped with goat cheese and chive-habanero rouille, with black bean and apple salad, *78,* 79
> octopus and mixed shellfish ceviche with sweet-and-spicy tomato broth, 37
> pan-fried, with parsnip puree and jícama salad, 80

P

Pancakes:
> black bean, *84,* 85
> sweet potato, 95

Panko, 27
Parsnip puree, 80

Pasilla (chile), *23,* 24
> emulsion, 191
> oil, 190–91
> sauce, 194

Pastel de coco y queso, 180, *181*
Pato:
> *carnitas de, 100,* 101, *196*
> *pechuga de, en mole de tamarindo,* 102–3
> *pozole de, 150,* 151

Pea shoot salad, 95
Pechuga:
> *adobada,* 148–49, *149*
> *con mole poblano,* 145
> *de pato en mole de tamarindo,* 102–3

Pepitas, halibut con, 4–5, 131, *132–33*
Pepper (bell):
> in broth, 136–37
> juice, 188
> red, coriander seed emulsion, 191
> red, habanero reduction, 189
> red, roasted, sauce, 196–97
> and tomato broth, spicy, 136–37

Pescado:
> *al chipotle,* 130
> *tiritas de, 74,* 75, *190*

Pesto, cilantro, 197
Phyllo:
> "corn husks," 170–71, *171*
> mushroom strudel, 166–67, *167*

Pico de gallo, 148–49, *149*
Pinto bean puree, 163
Pipian de puerco, 154, 155
Pipian sauce (pumpkin seed sauce), 200
> tamarind-rubbed pork tenderloin with, *154,* 155

Pirámide de res, 158
Plantain(s), *26,* 27
> puree, 76, 77
> sautéed, 145

Plátano, empanadas de, 172, 173
Poblano (chile), *23, 24,* 25
> mole, 199
> mole, grilled chicken breast with, 145
> potato and rajas gratin, 206
> roasted, sauce, 64–65
> roasted, stuffed with seafood and Gouda cheese, 72, *73*
> sopes with rajas, 98–99, *99*
> tomatillo broth, 32, *33*

Book designed by **Susi Oberhelman**
Production by **Kim Tyner**
Photographer assistants, **René López** and **Edgar Mejía**
Food stylists, **Laura Cordera** and **Leticia Alexander**
Prop stylist, **Mariana Hagerman**
Copy Editor, **Liana Fredley**
Proofreader, **Webster Williams**
Indexer, **Cathy Dorsey**

The text in this book was composed in
Akzidenz Grotesk
Designed by Günter Gerhard Lange in 1896
New Aster
Designed by Francesco Simoncini in 1958

Printed and bound in **Singapore**